Whe

In Civil Government

DANIEL NATION

Brandon L. Burden
FOREWORD BY CLAY NASH

Endorsements

Thank you, Brandon, for your efforts in the 88th Legislature to save Texas kids. I appreciate the busloads of grassroots patriots you brought to the Capitol to support the Ban Child Gender Modification Bill. Your presence was a tremendous shot of confidence for the representatives as they looked into the gallery and saw friendly faces counteracting the other side's intent to intimidate and threaten. Thank you for supporting my bill, and I hope your book is a smashing success.

Rep. Tom Oliverson, M.D.
Texas State Representative
House District 130

What a tremendous honor to recommend *Daniel Nation!* Daniel was selected by King Nebuchadnezzar not only because he was without blemish, of good appearance and skillful in all wisdom, endowed with knowledge, understanding, learning, and competent to stand in the king's palace, but because his Lord, our God, was with him!

Just like Pastor Brandon Burden is one of the Daniels of our day, so are "We the People." If we, as Christian Americans, will take a stand for our Lord God, He will fight all of our battles. If we lay the burdens of this great nation at the foot of the Father, He will fight on behalf of His righteous and obedient people.

Daniel Nation reminds us that this is our nation, and we have a civic responsibility to get engaged in the affairs of government so that we can see God transform people, families, leaders, cities, and our nation. As Pastor Brandon points out in *Daniel Nation,* the time is now for Christians to take back our government!

Member Evelyn Brooks
Texas State Board of Education
District 14

Daniel Nation is Pastor Brandon Burden's powerful testimony of what happens when Christians prayerfully and deliberately organize and engage in the legislative process. "We the People" have the God-given responsibility to engage in government, and are called to use our God-given gifts and talents to form His ekklesia. In the 88th Texas Legislative Session, we did this, and we witnessed the impossible be made possible through God's glory alone. *Daniel Nation* serves as an inspiration for future activism in the State of Texas and beyond.

Christin Bentley, M.S.
SREC Committeewoman Senate District 1
Republican Party of Texas

God's army, the ekklesia, is arising to push back and destroy evil powers that affect regions and territories! Brandon Burden in his powerful book, *Daniel Nation,* documents his journey to dismantle these high-level demonic spirits. Brandon started on his journey with only a desire to obey the first steps that he knew to do. You can do the same thing! The Holy Spirit led Brandon into unchartered waters! He experienced the strategy and power of God to overturn evil plots that would affect generations to come in his state.

Courage will arise as you read Brandon's book. You may discover your own call as part of the Daniel Nation!

Barbara Wentroble
President, International Breakthrough Ministries
Author and Speaker

Today, America is in desperate need of some Daniels who will speak out unafraid against the demonic tyranny that seems to be accelerating in this "One Nation Under God."

Like in the time of Hitler's Germany, we see American pastors falling into three categories: those who denounce the works of evil in our nation and are actively standing in the gap to bring America back to God, those who embrace and promote the works of evil, and those who stay silent. Sadly, most pastors have remained silent in America for decades.

For years I have prayed "God, get me to the remnant." He remains faithful to do just that! Pastor Brandon Burden is one of the Daniels of our day and I thank God for bringing us together on the battlefront. Our God is a God of hope. Pastor Burden brings us the strategy and hope that is needed today. If you want to be encouraged, this book is a must read!

Audrey Werner, R.N., B.S.N., M.A.
Founder, The Matthew XVIII Group
Dean of Life Issues at Masters International
University of Divinity

Renowned Bible Scholar, N.T. Wright, teaches there are two kinds of leaders in our world: (1) those who love power; and (2) those who have the power to love. Pastor and political activist, Brandon Burden, has written a stirring page-turner concerning the collision between these two kinds of leaders. His engaging and very informative book reads like a very dramatic novel, but trust me, his book is non-fiction!

The author has lived and experienced this collision which is currently going on in the culture and politics of our beloved nation! I cannot recall reading anything that is as compelling and activating as this volume! The message in these pages is informed by the revelation of the present and eternal kingdom of God and its agenda to impact and influence every sphere of life on planet Earth.

Though the author is focused on how to interact with civil government and influence it according to the standards of the Word of God, the truths he shares will educate and empower you to identify and labor to see the Gospel of Christ transform the

—

following: family, arts, media, entertainment, education, economy, etc.

Brandon's exciting journey will invite and equip you to be a kingdom leader who has the power to love and to be hope-filled about the future!

Jim Hodges
Founder and Leader
Federation of Ministers and Churches International

For years the challenge for Christians and conservatives has been knowing how to stop the encroaching political corruption devouring our nation. While the growing prayer movement has played a critical part in the war for America's destiny, many have been searching for what more they can do in this hour of battle. *Daniel Nation* is the first step to help answer that question.

Pastor Brandon Burden is both a man of great prayer and action! His inspiring true story will encourage you as you see how God is raising up an army of faith-filled believers who will both pray and show up on the political battlefield with love and truth to bring positive transformation to government.

It's time for our voices that are raised to heaven to also be raised on earth for the protection of the next generation. Pastor Burden is a true patriot and champion leading the way in an hour of fresh ekklesia movement. God bless you, Pastor Burden.

J. Nicole Williamson
Founder, King's Lantern Ministries

It's my privilege to recommend *Daniel Nation*! I have known Brandon Burden for many years, and now you, too, can tell that he is "the real deal" as a passionate Christian leader and culture shaper. The journey Brandon now shares with you in his book *Daniel Nation* will not just be good reading!

This book will inspire you as you follow Brandon's journey. He includes the times of frustration and opposition, which were always overcome by seeking God's strategies and hard work. *Daniel Nation* also gives you both spiritual inspiration and practical instructions for seeing true godly change not only in legislative policy but in the political system itself. Brandon's journey will empower you. May you be emboldened to be more involved in the governmental arena than ever before. *Daniel Nation* is a clarion call to YOU!

Bob Long
Rally Call Ministries
Rally Call Leadership Network

It is always an honor to be asked to endorse respected authors and their books. It is a double honor to do so for my son, Brandon. This book is not a written study of scripture and its relevant revelation for our time. It is the chronicle of real events, real people, the reality of the times in which we are living, and the warfare being waged for the preservation of the generations.

The story of Daniel is about a young Hebrew captive who was divinely placed into the court of Babylon to serve with his friends as an advisor to the king. From the position of influence, this company of influencers was strategically used by the Lord to shift the government mindset and ultimately the culture of that nation into the ways of Yahweh. Daniel established the kingdom of God in a culture that neither worshipped nor acknowledged Him as Lord and King.

Daniel Nation is the story about a company of devoted and dedicated followers of Christ who engaged the civil government of our state for the purpose of influencing civil leaders to enact laws that reflect the heart and righteousness of God. I was honored to serve in a small way in this assignment and am a witness to the events that are documented in this book. It is one thing to watch current events unfold on television news; it is quite another to be an eyewitness to those events firsthand.

I honor Brandon and the company of Daniels who wage spiritual warfare, the good fight of the faith, for the Father's purposes to become reality in our state and nation. May the influence of the Daniel Nation continue to hit the mark and reshape the future of coming generations in a healthy, wholesome, and godly way. May the God of our Lord Jesus Christ, the Father of glory, continue to give you the spirit of wisdom and revelation in the knowledge of Him in your forward press as Daniel Nation.

Larry Burden
Founder, Kingdom Life International
and Kingdom Life Apostolic Ministries

Brandon weaves a powerful retelling of how God moves through His people when they listen to His voice to act within the seven mountains of culture. This is not a tale of political action, but spiritual action in the political realm. As an eyewitness to many of the events mentioned in this book, I can attest to the amazing factual events that unfolded both in Frisco and Austin. *Daniel Nation* is a must-read!

Landon Atchison
Worship Pastor, Kingdom Life International
Frisco, Texas

As recorded in the Book of Matthew 24:1-51 (AMPC), Jesus' disciples asked this all-important question, "Tell us ... what will be the sign of Your coming, and of the end (completion, consummation) of the age?" (v. 3). He gave them several signs that we are experiencing this very day. One very important sign was this, "For the coming of the Son of Man (the Messiah) will be just like the days of Noah" (v. 37).

—

At that time the whole world was chaotic and had fallen so far from its original state that it required a total reset. Man had fallen into an all-time moral decay and completely lost his moral compass. That period sounds like the time we are living in now.

Here are a couple of questions that apply not only to the time of Noah, but relate to our current condition. Will the Son of Man find faith in the earth? Is it too late to reverse the amount of lawlessness and evil that exists? Yes, Noah found grace in the eyes of the Lord and was a righteous man in his world of total corruption. He built an ark of safety for his family and survived the flood.

The prophet Daniel spoke of a kingdom that was coming that would be established in these last days and would fill all the earth with the glory of the Eternal God just like it was before the Fall of Man in the Garden of Eden. At that time, Daniel was only a youth when he was taken captive into a Babylonian world system that ruled the whole earth. His lifestyle is a prototype of this twenty-first century Daniel Company that's arising today.

The fall and total destruction of this modern Babylon system is recorded in the Book of the Revelation of Jesus Christ. A company of Daniels is appearing once again at the most critical time in history when the devil is hell bent on destroying our youth, who are destined to play a major role in the preparation of the final appearing of the kingdom of heaven on earth.

These do not fear the threats of godless naysayers, like those in Daniel 3 when the edict went out saying you must bow to the image of anti-Christ spirits or else; you must not pray or ask any petition from any other god than the god of mammon of this world. The prophetic voices of the Daniel Generation are going to stand up in the face of evil like we have not seen since Noah's Day.

We need modern Daniels who will defy and overturn the court's rulings of anti-Christ spirits who have ruled this world far too long. Daniels who will stand firm and continue to pray to the God of Abraham, Isaac, and Jacob in the face of threats of demonic spirits who are parading in our city streets defying the Eternal Creator. Today's Daniels will not bow to idols nor compromise their faith even when threatened with facing the lion's den! I not only applaud, but highly endorse our spiritual son, Brandon Burden, and his no-compromise manifesto in our most critical time in history.

Samuel L. Brassfield
Harvest International Ministries, Inc.
Bertram, Texas

In reading *Daniel Nation,* it is obvious that Brandon is not just offering some firsthand information and experiences, but the reader is able to sense his burden for misled and misinformed people . . . of all ages. He shows us that Christians, sons and daughters of God, have a mandate from their heavenly Father to actively pray and be involved in the process of intervening and helping those who, quite possibly, don't even realize the depth and extent of help that they need in understanding the issues and meeting the challenges of our nation.

Brandon's book is an eye-opener that doesn't leave any Christian clueless as to one of the greatest and pressing needs in the history of our nation, nor does it leave any guessing as to where Christians are challenged to stand on such issues while they are even able to engage effectively in civil government for a righteous outcome.

I believe you would find it helpful and equipping, not only to read this book, but to also contact Brandon and accompany him on one of his group trips to the Capitol.

Marty Gabler
SEEC Ministries International
Coldspring, Texas

In Matthew 16, as Jesus was preparing to take His disciples into the most pagan region of the known world at that time – Caesarea Philippi – He asked them, "Who do you say that I am?" (v. 15). Peter answered, "You are the Christ, the Son of the Living God" (v. 16).

In response to that revelation answer, Jesus made what I believe to be the most powerful prophetic proclamation in the entire Bible ... "Upon this rock [truth], I will build My church [ekklesia]" (v. 18, clarification mine). The word ekklesia, simply defined, means "legislative assembly."

In other words, what Jesus was saying was that upon the truth of who He was, He was about to establish an assembly of people that would carry a legislative authority greater than that of any earthly form of government upon the face of the earth . . . the very authority of the kingdom of God!

Unfortunately, when King James authorized the translation of written scripture in the early 1600s, the word ekklesia was translated as church. In this translation, the Christ-prophesied governmental authority of God's people was veiled, and, today, we live under the consequence of that veiling . . . a weak, and getting weaker church!

In this book, Brandon Burden, doesn't just talk about the much-needed restoration of the Christ-prophesied ekklesia . . . HE DEMONSTRATES IT!

It was an honor to be a participant in the events he writes about, and I cannot stress enough how timely, relevant, and important I believe this book is to the Body of Christ in this hour of human history. I am honored to commend *Daniel Nation*.

EKKLESIA ARISE!

Kyle Byrd
Apostle, Front Line Ministries International
Founder and Senior Leader, The Epicenter

TABLE OF CONTENTS

Dedication

I want to dedicate this book to my wife, Willy, for her selfless love in allowing me to become the Daniel I am called to be. She stood by my side through relentless seasons of persecution and despair. She held my hand during my greatest victories and my darkest nights. She never once opened her mouth to retaliate against my enemies, even when she felt like it. Willy, you are my hero. I would not be who I am today without you.

Acknowledgments

I want to thank my wife and four kids for their support and sacrifice in my pursuit of becoming a Daniel in the mountain of civil government.

I want to thank my parents, Larry and Kathy Burden, for bringing me into this world, for constantly praying for me, and for always believing in me. You are the best parents a kid could ask for.

I want to thank my brother, Matthew, for always having my back no matter what.

I want to thank all the hard-working grassroots patriots, bus sponsors, and volunteers who made our mission in the 88th Legislature a smashing success.

I want to thank JoAnn Fleming and Grassroots America for honoring me with the 2023 Champion of Freedom award.

I want to thank Texas Scorecard for honoring me with the 2023 Texas Conservative Leader award. I would also like to thank Dr. Bob Koons for nominating me for this award.

I want to thank the North Texas Conservatives Board of Directors for their hard work and dedication in making our PAC a success.

I want to thank my church family for allowing me to fulfill my Daniel assignment while serving as their pastor, and for sticking by my side when the heat was on.

I want to thank those who defended my character and spoke up for me when I went through the media attacks of 2021. I will never forget those who wrote cards, left encouraging voicemails, prayed, and spoke words of life over me when I was in one of my darkest moments.

I want to thank Heidi Pezdek for submitting her eyewitness testimony of the Reverse the Kinsey Decision Day in the Old Supreme Court Room.

I want to thank the dozens of spiritual fathers and mothers who have poured into my life and taught me about the kingdom of God. There are too many of you to list, but you know who you are. I would not be where I am today without your love and support.

I want to thank Apostle Nicole Williamson and Sally May for helping me birth this book.

I want to thank my Lord and Savior, Jesus Christ, for saving me when I was twelve, filling me with the Holy Ghost when I was thirteen, and calling me into the ministry was I was fifteen. Without Jesus, I would have never made it this far in life. Thank you for every blessing you've given me. I love you with everything I am.

I want to thank all the Daniels who will read this book. May your calling to civil government burn like fire within you. May you arise and occupy this earth for Jesus Christ like never before! May my story be an inspiration to you, whether you are just getting started or are well on your way. The world needs you! Never let the devil convince you otherwise.

Foreword

"So the last will be first, and the first will be last" (Matthew 20:16, NIV).

There are those who lose and quit. There are those who lose and keep going—these are the ones who win the battle for they know that losing is merely a training ground.

Nothing worth doing is ever easy. Not at first. We are charting new territory and attempting things which have never been done before…at least not where we are, or under the circumstances we face. But God calls His people to frontiers; to the front tiers; to the places where Satan dwells; to the places where the Kingdom of God shall ultimately rule and reign.

Revelation 2:13 (NIV) says, "I know where you live—where Satan has his throne. Yet you remain true to my name. You did not renounce your faith in me, not even in the days of Antipas, my faithful witness, who was put to death in your city—where Satan lives."

Brandon Burden is a man called by God for greatness. Yet for the longest time, his life did not look like greatness. It looked like goodness. He married, raised children, and watched as his city of

Frisco, his state of Texas—indeed, the whole country—descended into moral decay at the instigation of politically connected activists.

At God's urging, Brandon decided to do something about it. He ran for local office. He poured his money and his life into the race. He staked his integrity and sacrificed his private life on the outcome of this battle that God had called him to.

And he lost.

Yes, he lost the local election. Worse, he watched the national election go the same way. Discouraged, he could have descended into his own loss, letting failure wrap him like a cloak as he absorbed the tsunami of regret and disillusionment.

But he didn't.

When God calls us, it is often not to an easy victory, but to train and to learn. Remarkable as it sounds, our losses in the small things are our training ground for victory in the great things. History bears this out.

Consider Abraham Lincoln—the president who was honored for turning the country away from human slavery:

- Lost his job in 1832.
- Defeated for state legislature in 1832.
- Failed in business in 1833.
- Elected to state legislature in 1834.

- Sweetheart died in 1835.
- Had nervous breakdown in 1836.
- Defeated for Speaker in 1838.
- Defeated for nomination for Congress in 1843.
- Elected to Congress in 1846.
- Lost renomination in 1848.
- Rejected for land officer in 1849.
- Defeated for U.S. Senate in 1854.
- Defeated for nomination for Vice President in 1856.
- Defeated for U.S. Senate in 1858.
- Elected President in 1860.

Lesser men and women quit in the process: *It's too hard. We have other priorities. Other challenges – those more manageable – call us here or there.*

This is the difference between a call to goodness and a call to greatness. We can live out our lives in the blessings of God, enjoying the fruit of the sacrifices of others … or we can step up, again and again, absorbing blow after blow, while each defeat makes us smarter, stronger, and more determined.

Training that doesn't first break us down cannot make us able to stand. Yes, God's call is to victory; we can see it from where we are. But between us and the glorious horizon is a rough and rocky trail.

Herein lies the genius of God. In calling us to battle – in leading us to victory – God strikes a blow not just at the immediate foe, but at the greater enemy: the entrenched forces who remain opposed to all He would do on the earth.

Our victories—small as they might seem—open channels in the heavenlies that affect more than our immediate circumstances. When we win an election or a legislative challenge, our victory establishes a precedent that remains in force long after we return to our everyday lives. Those people who come after us find the way open for their efforts.

"Who dares despise the day of small things, since the seven eyes of the Lord that range throughout the earth will rejoice when they see the chosen capstone in the hand of Zerubbabel?" (Zechariah 4:10, NIV).

Yet it's easy to overlook the positive impact our sacrifices make, isn't it? This is because a call to greatness does not look like greatness. It looks like hard work. It looks like defeat and discouragement. It looks like darkness. Why? Because darkness is where we take the battle.

Do you find yourself surrounded by the enemy? Rejoice. The day of God's preparation has arrived. Enemies will do what enemies do: attack. And God's people will do what they do: prevail and win ... eventually.

Brandon's story is one of eventual success, but that is not his message. His is one of perseverance and the preparation bestowed by defeat.

"Do not gloat over me, my enemy! Though I have fallen, I will rise. Though I sit in darkness, the Lord will be my light" (Micah 7:8, NIV).

Let us acknowledge the process set before us. Where there is a path, there is destination. Don't count small losses. They add up to great victories. When we start in the service of God, we enlist not only in His glory, but in the path that leads to glory.

People like to say that God calls us where we are. Yay! What quickly becomes apparent, however, is that where we are is the starting point, not the end point. It's the journey that qualifies us for the victory. It is our sacrifice that makes it possible.

"I want to know Christ—yes, to know the power of his resurrection and participation in his sufferings, becoming like him in his death, and so, somehow, attaining to the resurrection from the dead" (Philippians 3:10-11, NIV).

In this well written testimony, *Daniel Nation*, we learn a bit about people like Brandon—that rare breed who is not only called to restore the spiritual decay of our age but who faces it with God's Word. We have so much to learn because we have so much to do. Despise not small beginnings. They herald great outcomes.

May God bless you as you peruse these pages. May you stand in the arena to which God calls you.

Clay Nash
Clay Nash Ministries

"For the lovers of God may suffer adversity and stumble seven times, but they will continue to rise over and over again. But the unrighteous are brought down by just one calamity and will never be able to rise again."

Proverbs 24:16 (TPT)

Chapter 1

The Capitol Riot

Anxiety swept across my body as the protestors shouted in my face, "You hate me! You hate me!"

My stomach turned into knots. *This angry mob could tear me apart from stem to stern,* I thought. The truth, is I didn't hate anyone. I was trying to save Texas kids from the irreparable damage being done to children's bodies in the name of gender identity.

I was there at my state's Capitol in Austin, along with ninety-two other concerned believers who had come with me during Texas' 88th Legislative session, to fight for our children's protection against corrupt medical practices. Just two weeks earlier, I had attended a briefing with transgender survivors who had shared their horror stories of irreversible mutilations done to their bodies through gender modification drugs and surgeries.

I wasn't trying to take away anyone's rights, but I was trying to protect children from a lifetime of misery. I wasn't going to be silent and do nothing.

At 8:38 a.m. that morning, our group had arrived and were waiting for Senate Bill (SB) 14 to come to the floor. This bill, if passed, would prevent children under the age of eighteen from accessing procedures and treatments for gender transition drugs and treatments in the state of Texas. Its passage would also disallow the use of public money or public assistance for these purposes.

It was now 3:12 p.m. and just as the bill was about to be read, the voice of Democrat State Representative Mary González' rang out, "Point of order, Mr. Chairman! I raise a point of order against further consideration of Senate Bill 14 under Rule 4 Section 32 on the grounds the bill analysis is inaccurate and misleading."

"Please, bring your point of order down front," replied Speaker Phelan.

A hush fell across the audience as we awaited the Chair's decision. *Would the point of order be sustained or overruled?*

Suddenly, someone shouted, "One, two, three, four, trans folks deserve more."

Everyone focused their attention on a protestor who had made her way behind the Speaker's desk, continuing to yell her chant. As she did, others joined her. Suddenly, two protestors unfurled their banners and hung them off the balcony. One read, "Why are you soooo obsessed with me?"

It immediately became clear these protestors were intent on disrupting the proceedings. Texas Department of Public Safety (DPS) officers moved in and started to clear out the disruptors. We sat quietly in our seats, praying for calm.

A few moments later, however, Speaker Phelan declared from the podium, "Pursuant to the House constitutional authority, to prevent obstruction to these proceedings, the Chair orders the Sergeant at Arms to clear the gallery! The House will stand at ease until the gallery is cleared."

I couldn't believe what I was hearing! We had waited all day to hear this bill, and now we were asked to vacate the gallery before it could be heard. I slowly got up out of my chair and headed toward the door. The protestors, however, were refusing to leave. One protestor, a male, lifted his skirt and mooned the audience. I thought, *Oh, my God! Is this really happening?*

As I neared the door to the House gallery, a DPS officer yelled at me, "Get out of the way! Get out of the way!" Several officers moved past me, hauling off one of the protestors in handcuffs. At this point, I was in shock, making my way out of the gallery and into the hallway.

Angry protestors lined both sides of the hall chanting and screaming in our faces, "We're here. We're queer. We won't disappear!"

We shuffled by slowly trying to make our way out of the Capitol. The rotunda was a cacophony of lurid voices shouting in every direction.

"Protect trans rights! Protect trans rights!" the enraged mob screamed.

I tried to keep my eyes focused on the person in front of me as I placed one foot in front of the other. I prayed I could get everyone safely back on the buses without violence or bloodshed.

In that moment, I thought of the riot that took place in Ephesus in Acts 19: "Now when they heard this, they were full of wrath and cried out, saying, 'Great is Diana of the Ephesians!' So the whole city was filled with confusion, and rushed into the theater with one accord, having seized Gaius and Aristarchus, Macedonians, Paul's travel companions. Some therefore cried one thing and some another, for the assembly was confused, and most of them did not know why they had come together" (Acts 19:28-29, 32).

As I continued walking through the Capitol, I felt like I was living this Bible story in real time. Protestors continued to yell at me as I walked by in my red "Save Texas Kids" shirt.

Didn't they understand why I was there? Didn't they know what I was trying to do?

I wasn't trying to harm them. I was trying to save them—from themselves, if necessary.

———

No person in their right mind would do this to themselves. These kids were not in their right minds!

I continued around the third floor of the rotunda, trying to find the quickest way out. By now, I didn't know where the other ninety-two members of my group were located.

"Lord, protect them. Get them out of here safely," I prayed quietly.

The shouting persisted. I couldn't even hear myself think. "Lord, please guide me safely out of this building," I prayed.

I finally found the staircase to the east side of the Capitol and began to make my way down.

Chapter 2

How a Preacher
Entered Politics

The Bible says in Habakkuk 2:2, "Write the vision and make it plain on tablets that he may run who reads it." This Scripture has served me well throughout my life.

Since my teenage years, I have journaled much of what the Lord has spoken to me so I would remember it. This has included prophetic words I have received, prophetic words I have given, Scriptures I have studied, and revelation I have received in the secret place of prayer.

When I attended Bible college at seventeen, my understanding of Habakkuk 2:2 was greatly expanded. I learned that God's revelation was supposed to be written down so others could run with it, too. As I reflect on my journal writing, I realize that God has used it to develop a strategy that is defining my success in civil government today.

This successful strategy in my life has inspired me to write this book for Daniels who feel called to engage as Christians in civil government.

In 2018, the Lord spoke to me concerning a Daniel Company that would arise in the United States. He said, "I am raising an army of Daniels in the earth right now. They will go into the highest seats in the land. They will confront the Baals and the Ashtoreths. They will confront the spirit of Jezebel in the land. This is truly an unafraid generation. They are a young generation. They are the future. You are going to be amazed at what they do."

This prophetic word from the Lord accelerated a journey that I had been on since childhood. In the seventh grade, my gifted and talented teacher, Mrs. Hawthorne, required me to speak in front of the class for an assignment. After delivering my speech, she said, "Brandon, one day, you will either be a preacher or a politician."

Beaming from ear to ear, I said, "Thank you, Mrs. Hawthorne." I didn't realize then that she was referring to my booming voice and thunderous words, but I still consider it as a compliment.

Her encouraging words planted a seed of destiny within me that day. It was a seed that became a tree, as according to Isaiah 61:1, 3.

"The Spirit of the Lord God is upon Me, because the Lord has anointed Me to preach good tidings to the poor; He has sent Me to heal the brokenhearted, to proclaim liberty to the captives, and the opening of the prison to those who are bound. To console those who mourn in Zion, to give them beauty for ashes, the oil of joy for mourning, the garment of praise for the spirit of heaviness; that they may be called trees of righteousness, the planting of the Lord, that He may be glorified."

Heeding her words, I preached my first sermon in my dad's church when I was only thirteen years old. I remember exactly what the topic was: the baptism of the Holy Spirit.

My message was a barnburner! I discovered that preaching came quite naturally to me. It seemed easy to hold people's attention with my "booming voice and thunderous words."

Politics, however, was a much different story. That calling took time. God had to grab my attention to get me involved in the political arena. My initial wake-up call came when terrorists attacked America on 9/11.

I had always been a patriot at heart. I grew up at my grandfather's knees, listening to World War II hero stories as a kid. I was proud of my grandfather, who worked on the P-51 Mustangs that drove Hitler back to Germany. I was equally proud of my other grandfather, who jumped out of airplanes behind enemy lines.

I didn't know that grandfather very well because he was a peace officer who was killed in the line of duty when I was only seven years old. Nevertheless, I grew up listening to stories about him. He was the Andy Griffith of our town. Everyone looked up to him, including me. Having a hometown hero for a grandfather added to my sense of patriotism.

I also felt patriotic because of my three uncles who proudly served in the military. I even married a patriot! My wife served in the Air Force and was in inactive reserves the day terrorists attacked our country.

Though I was a patriot, like most other Americans I was asleep. On 9/11, however, I woke up. I knew that what had been done to our country was wrong. I knew that somebody was behind it, and I knew that they had to pay. I could feel the devil attacking our country from all directions, but I didn't know what to do.

Like many reading this book, perhaps you also sense the enemy's attack on our nation but don't know how to stop it. Maybe you feel overwhelmed, or perhaps you feel like it is a lost cause. Maybe you want to step up and do something, but you don't know what to do or where to start.

Well, I've got good news! God has a plan, and it involves you. So, keep reading. I pray you will feel encouraged as you do.

I didn't do much with my patriotic feelings between 2001 and 2014. During that time, I got married, had two kids, went back to college and earned my business degree.

I watched America go to war with Iraq and Afghanistan, I hung my American flag, and I attended the annual 9/11 and Veteran's Day ceremonies. I watched the news religiously until I got so disgusted with the passage of Obamacare that I cut my cable.

I helped a city council member run for re-election by hosting a meet and greet for him and hung out his campaign signs. I attended several city council meetings and supported a Political Action Committee (PAC) which defeated a 2 a.m. extended drinking hour law.

Eventually, I signed up for Leadership Frisco to learn how to become a community leader, but that was about as far as I took it. I did nothing more with my calling because I had never been taught how to engage in civil government as a Christian.

Then, God got my attention again in 2014. One night, I dreamed that a city council member stepped down from his position. In the dream, I ran into one of my classmates from Leadership Frisco who informed me they had found a replacement for him. My classmate said he tried calling me, but I didn't have my cell phone turned on. My name was on the list as a suitable replacement, but they had to keep going until they found someone else. The replacement was done hastily because the matter was urgent. Then, the dream ended. When I woke up, I recorded it in my journal but I didn't understand the dream's significance.

Two years passed and I hadn't thought about the dream again, until December 2016 when an email came across my desk from the city of Frisco. The email informed residents that a city council member had stepped down to run for mayor, and a special election was being held to replace his position.

The next day, I received an email from one of my friends saying, "Run for office, Bro!"

I emailed him back as a joke and said, "Haha! You run!"

Six days later, the city sent another email stating that the special election had been moved back one month to February. My same friend forwarded me the second email, to which I replied, "Saw it!"

Something started to stir within me, but it wasn't until several days later that I remembered the dream. I pulled out my journal from 2014, and to my amazement, it confirmed every detail of the city's email, including the name of the city council member who stepped down (as a side note, this is why journaling is so important!). I knew that God was speaking clearly, and I needed to listen.

I began taking steps towards filing for office. I met with the council member who was vacating his seat and asked him what he thought of my candidacy. Surprisingly, I received a favorable response.

He offered advice on creating push cards and gave me pointers on block walking (also known as canvassing). Push cards are printed collateral that tell voters who you are and why they should vote for you. Block walking or canvassing is knocking on doors to meet voters and ask for their vote. He also advised me where to get my campaign signs printed and how to create a list of voters to talk to. Overall, it was a positive conversation and I walked away feeling more confident with my decision.

Next, I printed the Candidate Application from the city's website and filled it out. But before I filed it, I wanted to ensure God was telling me to do it. You could say this was my "fleece moment" (Judges 6:36-40). So, five days before the filing deadline, I met with a group of seasoned ministry leaders to discuss my decision. I relayed the information about the dream and explained why I felt I was supposed to run. After praying together, we received confirmation from the Lord that I was supposed to do it. This further bolstered my confidence because I knew the Lord was in it.

After filing my candidate application, I immediately hit the ground running. I only had two months to campaign and had to figure out what to do. I had no name recognition. I had no real political connections, and I had no real game plan. All I had was a dream from the Lord.

The next step was filling out Candidate Questionnaires. I quickly learned that being a

43

candidate means everyone wants to interview you. I received questionnaires from groups like Frisco United and the League of Women Voters and news outlets like *The Dallas Morning News* and *Frisco Enterprise* magazine.

I filled out the questionnaires, answering them the best I could, but I started to recognize from their questions that I lacked real city council experience. I had never served on a board or a committee. I had never attended a city workshop. I had participated in several city council meetings, but that was about it. I quickly perceived I was entering a playing field where I would have to trust the Lord for every step.

The hardest part of being a candidate was attending the candidate forums. Even though speaking came naturally to me, the pressure of having to come up with answers to tough questions on the spot was unnerving.

My race was one of the largest in Frisco's history. Nine candidates ran for the seat as compared to a normal election where only four or five might run. One of the nine candidates was an incumbent. He had served on the city council for two terms and dropped off to run for State Representative. Losing his State Representative race, he decided to return and run for a third term on the city council.

This man had the name recognition, the money, and the experience. He also had the most endorsements, including the highly coveted Frisco

Fire Fighters Association. It indeed was a David versus Goliath story.

I'll never forget the Frisco Chamber of Commerce forum. At the end of the forum, candidates were allowed to ask one question of any other candidate. When it got to the incumbent, he asked laughingly, "Why are you all running against me?" We all laughed in response, but it was a good question.

This race was very different for Frisco politics. Never had city residents shown so much interest in an election. God revealed to me later that people were highly captivated by this election because He was trying to uncover something in our community.

One thing I have learned about God is that He will use a willing vessel when He needs to communicate a change in the earth. If you listen with prophetic ears, you can easily be the person that God uses to implement that change. This is what occurred in my election.

Frisco had been going down the path of a globalist city for years. One of our previous mayors had gone overseas and courted globalist companies to move to Frisco. He wanted Frisco to become the next Dubai, a city fueled by foreign investment. He desired to urbanize our city with Class A office space and dense mixed-use developments, which would double our population, not to mention the traffic congestion.

Frisco's infrastructure wasn't designed to handle such growth, but this leader did not care. He wanted his vision at any cost. The problem was that nobody would stand up and challenge this notion.

When I entered the race, my platform centered on lowering the density in Frisco by limiting the number of future urban and multi-family apartment developments. At the time, Frisco had doubled its permits for apartment construction and changed its land use plan to allow for even more. The projected program called for 58,500 urban units, not to mention 7,150 multi-family units at full build-out. This would result in a projected population of 374,840.[1] At the time, our population was around 170,000.

The problem with Frisco's plan was that they had failed to prepare for the gridlock that 374,840 residents would bring. I'll never forget the day the city announced that a *flying Uber* would be our solution. The newspaper released images of heliports at Frisco Station where passengers could Uber through the air.

I thought, *there's no way I'd ever let a taxi fly me through the air*. Then, another time, a scooter company dropped off their scooters throughout the city. They said they were testing the Frisco market.

I laughed hysterically at the thought of taking a scooter several miles into downtown Frisco. Our city had no bike paths from my house to downtown. Our sidewalks didn't connect because of undeveloped land in between the subdivisions. Then there is the issue of riding a scooter in 100-degree Texas heat

—

with 80% humidity! Scooters just didn't make sense and the ludicrousness of this proposition inspired me to make a funny video about it.

The Lord then gave me a strategy of making videos to reach voters with my ideas about lowering density. Videos weren't popular yet for informing voters about local government issues, but following the Lord's strategy allowed me to reach thousands of residents quickly and efficiently.

One of my videos, shot in front of a recently developed apartment complex, went viral and received over 25,000 views. This propelled me to the front of the race, resulting in my coming in second place on Election Day. My opponents were completely surprised by the results and I was, too. I didn't expect to be dead last, but I didn't expect to be in second place, either.

The next day, I received a call from the incumbent. He asked if I would concede the race in exchange for a city board position. He told me that my runoff would cost the city thousands of dollars and that I should concede the race to save the city money.

This was the greatest challenge of my campaign as it was a very enticing offer. I went back to the group of ministry leaders who had initially prayed with me, and I asked them for their advice. I received a resounding, "No!" from all of them. They said that to accept the board position would be disobedience to what the Lord had initially asked me to do.

47

I declined the offer and told the incumbent that I would continue my campaign against him. The runoff election was even more grueling than the primary. I only had thirty days to figure out how to win.

Funds weren't a problem at this point. I now had name recognition, and I also had support from the PAC, Frisco United. My problem, however, was how to get voters to turn out. Voter fatigue is very high because so many elections are held yearly in Frisco. Typically, runoff elections see a meager turnout. How would I motivate fatigued voters to come to the polls, again?

Frisco is a large city—approximately seventy square miles. How would I canvass enough doors to reach these voters? I was in a quandary. My Campaign Manager told me to keep making videos because they would be enough to get me across the finish line. Conventional wisdom said I needed to canvass, but I needed a team to help me and I didn't have those resources.

Fortunately for me, the incumbent took a vacation during the runoff. He wasn't worried about losing. He had garnered 45.72% of the vote in the primary as compared to my 18.57%. I, on the other hand, had to work furiously if I was going to win.

I made more videos and sent them to hundreds of my supporters, requesting they share them relentlessly. I canvassed as much as I could with my dedicated team of two – my mom and me. We block walked all seven hundred homes in Frisco Lakes, a massive senior living community with high voter turnout. I attended more meet and greets. I hosted an enormous get-out-the-vote rally at Frisco Heritage Center the night before the election, asking voters to bring their neighbors to the polls on Election Day. I did everything that I knew to do to campaign.

I know what you expect me to say next—that I won my race and lived happily ever after. Well, that's not what happened. I lost. I had an impressive turnout, garnering 44.9% of the vote, but I failed to cross the 50% threshold needed to win.

I had gained 26% new voters from the primary but it wasn't enough. I beat the incumbent with more votes on Election Day, but he beat me during early voting. I only lost by 432 votes, but a loss is still a loss.

I received positive affirmation from other city council members for my efforts, but ultimately, I didn't win. In a world where everything is based on winning and losing, I, my friends, was the loser. This was a tough pill for me to swallow.

At the time, I believed that if God called you to do something, you would always be successful— EVERY SINGLE TIME! I thought with God all things are possible. I believed that with God I could do all things through Christ. I felt that anything I asked in His name would be done. The truth is that I had a lot of growing up to do. My campaign was a huge learning experience that taught me a lot about people and even more about God.

The primary thing I learned through my campaign is that with God, it is always about obedience first and foremost. God continually tests our hearts to see if we will do what He asks us to do. He is looking for willingness, not success.

Why does God view it this way? Because our obedience opens our hearts to Him, creating agreement with His plans. God needs our agreement for His kingdom to come and His will to be done on the earth. As a matter of fact, He can do nothing without our agreement.

The Bible says in Psalm 115:16 (TPT), "The heavens belong to our God; they are His alone, but He has given us the earth and put us in charge." God has given man stewardship rights over the earth. Without our agreement and cooperation, He cannot do what He wants to do when He wants to do it.

Contrary to popular belief, God is not in control of the earth; man is. According to Merriam-Webster's Dictionary, the word control means "to have power over; rule." Rule is defined as "control of, or dominion over an area, or people." In Genesis 1:28, when God said, "Let them have dominion over the earth," He was speaking to mankind. God is sovereign, but mankind is in control, according to Scripture.

———

We are free-will managers with agency over His creation. He depends on us to cooperate with His plans and purposes because our obedience shifts the earth into agreement with His will.

The second thing I learned through my campaign is that God will use your *seeming* failures to fulfill His will. God wanted to address the high-density issue in Frisco using me as His mouthpiece. It wasn't about me winning the race. It was about me becoming an influencer who shaped the mayor's race.

Frisco was always a single-family-residence-focused suburb of Dallas. Thousands of families moved to Frisco for its school district, affordable housing, and nice suburban feel. However, in the years leading up to my campaign, Frisco quickly changed into an urban-metro feel. God wanted to say something about that. He wanted to bring Frisco's plans for a high-density build-out into the public eye. He also wanted to build a platform for residents to voice their concerns with city leaders because they weren't listening to residents at city council meetings.

Many residents found their voice through my platform. My campaign was so effective that it impacted the mayoral race held one month later. The two candidates were forced to address the high-density issue in Frisco, and both made campaign promises to lower the density, if elected.

The third thing I learned through my campaign is that we often don't understand God's higher purpose in asking us to do something. When we say, "Yes" to God, it opens doors for us that will accomplish a higher purpose in our future. The rest of this book will speak to what happened in my life because of my simple obedience to run for city council.

Even though I didn't get the desired results in my election, the doors it has opened have been astounding. I hope that you will stay with me through the remaining pages. I have some exciting stories and some decisive victories to share!

The final thing I learned through my campaign is that you can be whoever God has called you to be. When Mrs. Hawthorne planted that seed within me in the seventh grade, my religious mindset told me I could only be a preacher or a politician. I didn't know that in God's kingdom you can be both. In this hour, God is calling us to step out of our religious thinking and imagine what is possible in the kingdom.

Maybe God wants to use you to break old mindsets that keep people bound. Perhaps, He wants to use you as a Joseph in business, or a Daniel in civil government. Maybe you are destined to do great and mighty exploits for God in your generation (Daniel 11:32).

I tell you, my friends, all things are possible in God. I'm about to share some exploits that God has done through me. I pray my story will encourage you to do some exploits, too!

Chapter 3

The Government of God

After my city council defeat, I was crushed. I felt like God had let me down. I didn't understand why He didn't let me win. I had the momentum behind me and felt like I would ride the wave to victory. I just ran out of runway. Thirty days wasn't enough time for me to campaign. I always felt like I would have won if I had just one more week.

I blamed myself for not doing more with the dream in 2014. Had I discerned it accurately, I would have realized it was a preparatory dream. I might have worked harder to attend more city council meetings and workshops. I may have tried to get on a board or committee. I would have studied harder to learn how local government works. I would have made more political connections to position myself in the city.

In hindsight, though, I don't believe I was ever meant to win that race because I didn't understand the power behind the political spirit or the political system at the time. I would have come entirely under its control if I had won my election. Just that one phone call with the incumbent asking me to compromise showed me how close I came to succumbing to its plans.

The political spirit is one of compromise. It is a spirit where everybody is in bed with everybody politically and financially (and sometimes, physically, too!). It is a spirit whereby you must sell your soul to the devil to get ahead.

It can be compared to the same spirit in corporate America, where you either compromise your values to get to the top or step on everybody's head to get what you want.

The political spirit is married to the corporate spirit. They are both fueled by greed and ambition. There is a term for it in the Bible called mammon. In Matthew 6:24, Jesus said, "You cannot serve both God and mammon."

Mammon is defined here as riches. You cannot serve the world's riches and enticements and God simultaneously. It doesn't mean that you can't have wealth or riches. It just means that they can't have you.

Politics is a system ruled primarily by Baal and Jezebel worship. Baal is a principality that goes by a thousand different names. It was the primary god worshipped by the Canaanites and was believed to be a fertility god who helped the earth produce crops, and help people have children. In ancient

Babylon, Baal worship involved lewdness, bloody orgies, human sacrifice, and ceremonial prostitution.[1]

Jezebel was a Phoenician priestess who married Ahab, the king of Israel. She saturated Israel with the worship of Baal and the goddess Asheroth (Baal's wife). Jezebel's chief sway was the seduction of God's people, especially the rulers and leaders of Yahweh, to her father's gods.[2] Through Jezebel's influence, Israel turned away from God and worshipped idols on every high hill. They even sacrificed their own children to the god Molech.

If you study the Seven Mountains of Culture taught by Lance Wallnau, you will realize that Satan seeks to dwell on the mountain of government. The Seven Mountain teaching is a strategy for evangelism that was developed by Loren Cunningham, founder of Youth With A Mission (YWAM). Loren was praying in 1975 about how to turn the world around for Jesus. The Lord revealed to him seven areas that, if focused on, would turn the world around for God.

These areas included religion, family, education, government, media, arts and entertainment, and business. The day after his revelation, Loren was having lunch with Bill Bright, founder of Campus Crusade for Christ, whom God had also given a similar Seven Mountain strategy. In his revelation, the Lord told Bill that there were seven mountains, or kingdoms, to take that were the mind-molders of society.

The Lord instructed each of them to tell the other this message at lunch, along with an important promise that if we captured these mountains, we'd capture the nation.[3] In 2000, Lance Wallnau came along and expanded the message after Loren shared the revelation with him. Lance views the Seven Mountains as mind-molders that influence world kingdoms through strongholds that Christians must take dominion over.[4]

Some have labeled this teaching as dominion theology or Christian nationalism. I, and others who I run with, call it the dominion mandate, as given to mankind in Genesis 1:28.

Satan had to strategically choose which mountain of culture he wanted to be on because he could only be in one place at one time. So, why did Satan choose the civil government mountain? Primarily because civil government is the sphere where we disciple nations.

Think about it. We make the laws here. We print the money here. We set the standards for living here. We interact with other countries here. What better place to transfer our ideals and culture to others? I wish Christians truly understood what mature discipleship looks like as it relates to the Seven Mountains of Culture! Satan understands this concept so much better than we do.

In Matthew 28:19, Jesus told us to "Go therefore and make disciples of all the nations, baptizing them in the name of the Father and of the Son and of the Holy Spirit." Christians interpret this Scripture as meaning we should make converts or proselytes. However, there is so much more meaning to this verse.

In our narrow view, we have focused most of our efforts on witnessing when we should be focused on both witnessing and influencing. We have focused our efforts on mentoring, while Satan has focused his efforts on fathering evil. We've focused on bringing people into the church, while Satan has focused on capturing people in the marketplace. We have been writing songs while Satan has been writing laws. We have been entertaining people while Satan has been empowering people. We have been creating platforms for ministry while Satan has been creating policy for nations.

If we only understood that, in its fullest context, the Great Commission is about who is reigning and ruling over culture!

In a nutshell, the kingdom is about taking dominion or legislating over the earth. Jesus legislated everywhere He went by demonstrating the kingdom to others. When sickness came before Him, it had to leave. When demon-possessed people hissed and screamed at Him, the demons had to flee. When the spirit of death challenged him, death had to yield up the grave.

When religious leaders tried to subvert His authority, they had to yield, too! Nothing and no one could stand before Jesus. Everything had to bow in submission to His authority. Why? Because Jesus understood the kingdom, which means that He understood dominion.

Christians must understand dominion if we are to disciple nations. God has a government, and we are part of it. We are not political, but we are governmental! We serve the highest government of all — the government of God.

The government of God trumps all human government. It trumps every evil government. It trumps every tyrannical government. It also trumps every other spiritual government.

Did you know that sickness is a spiritual government? It is a spiritual government that wants to destroy your mind and body. It is a spiritual government that controls your thoughts. It is a spiritual government that controls your emotions. It is a spiritual government that controls your body.

You can easily see this government in action when you get sick. Everything tends to come under its control as the symptoms appear. Yet Jesus easily destroyed the government of sickness in people's bodies. Why? Because He exercised a higher level of spiritual government — the government of God.

Everything God does is governmental, meaning that everything He does points to His reign and rule.

The Bible says that God is over all (Ephesians 4:5-6). He owns all of the gold and the silver (Haggai 2:8). He owns all of the cattle on a thousand hills (Psalm 50:10). He owns everything in heaven and on earth (Deuteronomy 10:14).

Nowhere in Scripture do I see where Satan owns anything. I see where he might have stolen some things, but I don't read where God gave him anything.

Many Christians have been taught that the earth is under the mark of the beast, the false prophet, and the anti-Christ, so we're supposed to give up our planet because that's the only way Jesus can return. That, my friends, is just simply not true. We aren't supposed to give anything to Satan.

Christians have also been taught that everything on planet Earth is under God's control. We should expect God to do everything for us because, after all, He is in charge. We believe that everything that happens occurs because God allows it. We believe that everything first passes through His hands and must be permitted.

What if I told you that was erroneous thinking? What if I told you that these two concepts are both immature and incomplete?

What if I told you that you had a part to play in Earth's events and that your part might determine the outcome?

What if I told you that you are a part of a heaven and earth partnership?

What if I told you that the devil was the one causing all the havoc, and we have the power to stop it?

Would you pray differently?

Would you think differently?

Would you engage in faith differently?

I believe you would!

I wonder, though, if you have ever been told the truth. Earth does not belong to Satan or his minions. God cast Lucifer down to Earth like lightning, sometime between Genesis 1:1 and Genesis 1:2. But just because he was cast down doesn't mean he was given rights to the earth. No!

On the contrary, he had to deceive man into usurping his rights because those rights weren't his in the first place. Subsequently, the Bible tells us that Jesus restored those rights when He died on the cross (Ephesians 4:8-10). Most Christians, however, have been taught that Jesus only died for one reason: to save our souls and take us to heaven. We barely teach anything about the original package of rights that were restored.

Our going to heaven is only part of the reason Jesus died. The other part involves full restoration of the earth and our dominion over it.

What if I told you that everything Satan destroyed, Jesus died to restore? What if I told you that, in addition to our salvation, Jesus died to restore the earth back to its original design?

What if I told you that, in the days ahead, the earth would look more garden-like and less hell-like? What if I told you that we don't have to wait for Jesus to return to start ruling and reigning over the earth? What if I told you that we could start right now?

That is what Daniel Nation is all about—ruling in the midst of our enemies and bringing order to the chaos. Daniels are called to rule in the midst of disorder, bring clarity to the confusion, and release peace in the midst of cultural unrest. Our job is to manifest heaven on earth.

God sent Satan to the earth to punish him for his deeds. He didn't send him down here on vacation. God instituted the system for this punishment when He created Adam to rule over the earth.

In Genesis 1:28, God told man to be fruitful and multiply, to fill the earth and subdue it, and to have dominion over every living thing that moves on it. The Hebrew word for dominion is *radah*, which is defined as to rule, subjugate, trample, tread, or dominate.[5]

Used in context, the word means to prevail against, reign, or take over. When God put man in charge of the Garden in Genesis 3:15, He expected him to *radah* upon His behalf. This included *radah-ing* over the wild animals, the birds in the sky, the fish in the sea, and even Satan himself.

Genesis 3 tells us that Satan came in the form of a serpent and deceived man. Had Adam remembered his mandate to *radah* over the serpent, this story would have had a much different ending. However, Adam gave his authority to *radah* over to Satan by heeding the serpent's words. Adam allowed Satan to take dominion over the earth. Satan bruised our heel in this exchange, but it was not a permanent arrangement.

Jesus came thousands of years later to crush Satan's head as prophesied in Genesis 3:15. When Christ died on the cross, He defeated Satan once and for all, making him the forever loser according to Colossians 2:15. We became the victors through Christ, and in our redeemed state, we are constant reminders of Satan's permanent defeat.

We enforce Satan's defeat by crushing his works daily through the name of Jesus and the power of His blood. Every time one of God's beloved children accepts the blood of Jesus for their redemption, they crush Satan's head. Every time one of God's beloved children prays in the name of Jesus, they crush Satan's head.

Every time one of God's beloved children wields the authority of the Word of God, they crush Satan's head. Satan is punished over and over again as we

---

enforce Christ's victory bought and paid for at the cross.

Satan, however, has flipped the script on many Christians. He has deceived many into believing he has authority over the earth. He has convinced many Christians that heaven is our home and that the earth belongs to him. This has created a mindset in many believers where we are just passing through this life waiting for the next.

Many Christians already have their rapture suits on and can't wait until the day Jesus comes back and takes care of Satan for us. Well, I've got news for you! Jesus already did that.

According to Colossians 2:15, Jesus defeated Satan once and for all on the cross 2,000 years ago. "Having disarmed principalities and powers, He made a public spectacle of them, triumphing over them in it."

Nowhere do I read in Scripture that Jesus has to come back and do that job again. Also, nowhere do I read that Jesus has to come back in the rapture and rescue us from Satan's clutches. What I do read in Matthew 28:18 is that all power has been given to Jesus in heaven and on Earth, and through the power of the Holy Spirit given in Acts 2:1-4, we have received the same power He walked in.

I also read in Matthew 16:19 that He has given us keys to bind and loose on the earth. Keys speak of authority to lock and unlock things in our realm.

I also read in Luke 10:19 where it says that Jesus has given us authority to tread on serpents and scorpions and over all the power of the enemy. It doesn't say over SOME power of the enemy — it says over ALL power of the enemy. If I am interpreting Scripture correctly, what this tells me is that Satan is under our feet, not vice versa. To me, that sounds a lot like we're in charge of things, not Satan.

Why are we living like a bunch of defeated Christians trying to escape the earth through the rapture? Why are we nervous every time the Centers for Disease Control (CDC) announces a new COVID-19 variant that's supposed to kill us? Why do we get scared when terrorists threaten us with global takeover? Why do we fear our government and what evil leaders can do to us?

"God has not given us a spirit of fear, but of power and of love and of a sound mind" (2 Timothy 1:7).

If we understood that we have dominion over Satan every day, we would resist all of the weapons he has formed against us. We would not put up with anything he says he is going to do to us. We must come to an understanding that heaven is advancing, and hell is retreating. The war has already been won. Satan knows this and is scared. As we learn and walk in this truth, he grows scared of us, too.

We need a mindset of victory in this hour. Yes, our final dominion will come when Jesus returns, but that doesn't mean we can't take command over the earth right now. Jesus said, "Occupy till I come" (Luke 19:13).

Jesus is coming back for a reigning, ruling church that knows how to occupy planet Earth! He is not coming back for a wimpy bride. He is returning for a mature bride who is reigning and ruling over the nations. After all, isn't our life here on Earth just a warm-up for when He returns?

Revelation 20:4 says we will reign and rule with Him for a thousand years. One thousand in Scripture is a number that represents an indefinite amount of time, or full maturity. In other words, we will reign and rule with Christ forever.

Don't you think that God, in His infinite wisdom, would prepare us for such an essential task before His Son returns? Well, the good news is, He is! He is teaching us how to take dominion daily as we enforce Christ's victory over Satan.

As you read this chapter, I pray that something leaps inside your heart. I pray that something rises within you and says, "You know what? Brandon, you're right!" Why am I acting defeated, like the devil has all this power over planet Earth when God says we are the victors and Satan is the forever loser? Why have I believed that I can only reign and rule after Jesus returns? Why can't I do it right now?

If you catch what I am teaching here, you will understand what the Daniel Nation movement is all about. Daniel Nation is about advancing the

67

kingdom of God throughout the earth as we dispossess Baal and Jezebel's reign. The move of God that is coming will re-establish our dominion mandate (Genesis 1:28), resulting in a reigning and ruling bride.

In 2023, the Lord gave me this prophetic word:

> "Tell My people that this nation will no longer bow its knee to Baal. I am done with Baal worship in this land. I AM DONE WITH IT! I will permit it no more! Baal's cup of iniquity has reached its fullness and is overflowing. I have heard the cries of My people, and I am releasing them from their bondage as a result of Baal worship. I am throwing down Baal. I am throwing down Jezebel. I am rooting up, and I am routing out all of the underground caverns of the enemy. The enemy has come out of his hiding place, and there is no more safety for him there. He is exposed. He is weak. He is helpless, and he cannot defend himself. Can the enemy defend himself against the Almighty? I say NO!"

Can you hear the directness in God's voice? I can. There's a sense of imminence and immediacy to it. God is done with evil on planet Earth. He is not going to permit Baal worship any longer.

God will no longer stand by while innocent children are slaughtered in the name of Molech worship. He will no longer turn away while children are sex trafficked in this nation. He is done with Satan's agents peddling power for blood sacrifice on the trading floor of humanity.

God is shaking evil loose in our lifetime because He wants to demonstrate His power to this generation. He is tired of us being ignorant of the devil's devices. He is tired of us falling for Satan's schemes. He wants to rise within us and empower us to push evil out of our land.

The Lord also spoke this to me in 2023:

"It is time for My people to rise. It is time for My people to take the land. It is time for my people to trim their wicks and be ready. For I will come quickly. I will come quickly, I say, and My people must be ready. Tell my people not to be sleeping on the job. Don't be like my disciples in the garden who fell asleep when I needed them most. I need My people to be on the job. Their job is to see what I'm doing, agree, and decree it upon the earth. My people are to manifest My glory. I am coming to swallow up the earth in My glory. The earth shall be filled with My glory as the waters cover the seas."

The quick coming the Lord is referring to is not the Parousia (the second coming). What He is referring to is the coming of His glory tsunami. What He is saying is that His manifest presence (or glory) is about to swallow up this earth and everyone will feel it. Everyone will see it. Everyone will sense it. God is about to move like we have never seen Him move before.

You can be a part of this move of God. You don't have to be on the outside looking in. You can be on the inside looking out. The kingdom of God is like a participation sport. God doesn't believe in benchwarmers. Let the Spirit of God rise within you today. Ask Him to activate you. Ask Him to get you into the fight. It's a lot of fun! Just read the next chapter.

Chapter 4

How a Brainchild Was Born

After my run for the city council, my friends and family told me not to stop. They probably sensed my deep discouragement and lack of desire to try anything new because of my loss.

Once I finally pulled myself back together, I rebooted my mission by becoming a voice in the community. I attended almost every city council meeting. I went to planning and zoning meetings. I attended city workshops. I went to town hall meetings, and continued to follow high-density projects in the city and make videos about them.

I called city council members out when they said one thing during their campaign, but then voted another way on issues. I even signed up for, and graduated from, Frisco Citizen's Police Academy and Frisco Citizen's Fire Academy.

The main point is that I didn't go away. I stayed plugged in, which was a decision that postured me for success in the next leg of my journey.

I ascertained that what I needed to do after my election was to get on a board. I applied for city boards and commissions, but was denied multiple times as political retribution for my council run. I was "too dangerous," as they put it.

Technically, I was very dangerous to the mayor's high-density plans. Even though he came out with a campaign advertisement saying that density mattered to him, the first thing the council did under his new leadership was vote for two high-density projects.

I was there the night the vote took place; it is a matter of public record. Knowing I would not get on any city boards or commissions, I did the next best thing and I got on my HOA board.

I didn't do much politically for the next two years beyond serving on this board. My wife and I got pregnant with our third child, which took up much of our time. I also went to real estate school and became a REALTOR®. That also took up a lot of my time. I continued to lead a movement in Frisco focused on fighting the increase in urban density, however, I did it in small group meetings with city residents, pastors, church groups, and parents of Frisco Independent School District (FISD) kids.

I listened to their concerns about the impact the growth of urban density would have on our school system. Would it bring in a transient community? Would it increase crime? Would it lower the quality of education? There was also a concern about high taxes in our city. The issue of rising property taxes arose during my campaign and continued to be a problem after my race ended. Inflated property taxes were affecting me, too! My wife and I built a new home in 2014, and within three years, our property taxes were eating us alive.

My next big political move came in 2019 when I got involved in the 86th Texas Legislature to lobby for property tax reform. I'll never forget speaking in front of a committee for the first time. It was the Senate Committee on Property Tax chaired by Senator Paul Bettencourt. I was so nervous.

I sat in the committee hearing all afternoon, waiting to be called. I grew more nervous as I witnessed committee members go toe to toe with witnesses. I thought, *Oh, Lord! Senator Bettencourt is going to chew me to bits.*

When it was my turn to speak, the senator had to leave the room to check in with the finance committee. I viewed this as the providence of God and my heart shouted for joy. He appointed Vice Chair Angela Paxton to preside in his absence.

I relaxed a little bit because I knew Senator Paxton from the district. I met her in Collin County at a campaign event, and she was cordial to me. With a sigh of relief, I began my testimony, "Hi, my name is Brandon Burden, and I'm representing myself. I'm here today because I attended an online Frisco Town

73

Hall meeting on Tuesday night. When I heard that the mayor of Frisco opposed this bill, I felt I had to come here as a resident to speak in favor of it."

I then testified how my property taxes had risen 76% since moving to Frisco. I continued, "With a property tax cap in place like the one proposed in SB 2, residents wouldn't be in the situation we were currently in." After concluding my testimony, Senator Paxton responded graciously, stating that she also lived in my area and felt the tax burden personally. I was so glad she didn't ask me any questions! I honestly wasn't sure if I could have answered them.

Later that session, SB 2 passed. Known as the Texas Property Tax Reform and Transparency Act of 2019, it made sweeping overhauls to the state's property tax system. The new law required voter approval before local governments increased their property tax revenue by more than 3.5%. A massive win for property owners, this bill was the first victory toward significant property tax relief in Texas in many years.

I was so proud to be a part of the process of crafting good legislation in Texas. It validated the hard work I put into my city council race, and I felt like my voice was truly heard for the first time.

After attending the legislative session, my next move was to help one of my campaign supporters with his re-election to the Frisco school board. He

—

had helped my campaign tremendously by connecting me with his supporters, and when he announced his re-election campaign, I decided to help him. He was running against an opponent that Frisco schoolteachers supported, and it was a very tough race.

Even though a group of us worked hard for his re-election, he lost. It was a loss we all took very hard. Twelve of us gathered at a café in Frisco to debrief about the election. The mood at our table, to say the least, was very gloomy. Many of us were long-time Frisco residents and were disillusioned with the city's direction. Quite frankly, we were now asking ourselves if we wanted to move away or stay and fight a bit longer.

As we went around the table that morning, the consensus was that we wanted to try and fight one more time. This battle cry became the starting point for our brainchild: Frisco Conservatives.

Frisco Conservatives PAC was created to push back against the cabal in Frisco. In political terms, the cabal is the clique or faction that controls government. President Trump called it the "deep state." Whatever you want to call it, it became apparent while under Trump's Presidency that a secret faction is running this country.

Some players are obvious. Others are not. For our city, we defined the cabal as those who wanted FISD's policies to look more like Chicago and the city council's policies to look more like San Francisco. We were determined to change this leftist direction in our city.

At one of our first roundtables, we brought in a city councilman from Plano who had pushed back against high-density apartments and won. He became one of our biggest cheerleaders, helping us find the path to victory.

The strategy behind Frisco Conservatives was quite simple. We discovered that 15,000 Republicans voted in Frisco's 2016 presidential primary but didn't vote in our municipal elections. We believed we could beat the cabal if we could reach those voters with our candidates for city council and school board.

We also discovered that conservatives were losing elections in Frisco because there was a 45% vacancy rate in Republican precinct chairs on the Denton County side, and a 50% vacancy rate on the Collin County side. Without precinct chairs, we weren't going to win any races, so it became very important to find a way to fill these vacancies.

The Lord gave us a witty idea for filling these chairs. One night, a small group of us sat down and looked at all the precincts in Frisco. We identified the vacant precincts as well as the precincts that cabal members chaired, and we made a list of all these precincts. Then, we went through our databases and came up with names of people who lived in those areas. We added those names to our list and started reaching out to them.

The holidays were approaching, and one of our PAC members lived in a gorgeous home in Frisco. So, we invited our recruits to a Christmas party at his house. God instructed us to have precinct chair applications ready at the party and a notary present to notarize them. As our recruits entered the house, we made them stop at the front door, fill out an application and get it notarized. By the end of the evening, we had around twenty notarized applications (including my own).

The next day, we dropped off the applications with the appropriate county offices, well in advance of the filing deadline. Most of our applicants weren't faced with opponents and filled their vacancies immediately by being voted in at a County Executive Committee (CEC) meeting. Those who did face cabal opponents beat them in the primary.

By March 2020, we had filled all but three vacant precincts in Collin County and all but one in Denton County, which resulted in a 93% occupancy rate in our city. These new precinct chairs became the key to building our army.

Our next big task was electing a new chairman for the Republican Party of Texas (RPT). Most of us were unhappy with the current chairman. When we learned that the state convention was only months away, we became delegates to our Senatorial District

(SD) conventions. The SD convention is held on the fourth Saturday after the primary. Anyone may attend the convention as a guest, but only those elected by their precinct can be delegates.

Delegates to the convention consider and vote on resolutions, then elect delegates and alternates to the state convention. We all wanted to become delegates to the state convention because Lieutenant Colonel Allen West had thrown his name into the hat and was running for state chair.

The first time I met Allen West was at a winter gala held by Empower Texans on December 7, 2019. The first thing he said to me was that I was wearing my American flag on the wrong lapel. He took my pin off my right lapel (without asking, I might add) and put it on my left lapel (yes, he did!) He said, "You always wear the American flag over your heart."

That was my introduction to Allen West. I must say that I felt genuinely humbled in the presence of greatness. I could tell from the moment I met him that he was a true patriot. So, needless to say, when Allen threw his name in the ring to run for state chair, I was behind him all the way.

The 2020 Republican State Convention was the convention that never started (well, it barely started). It took place during the outbreak of COVID-19 when the world was topsy-turvy. The city of Houston told the party at the last minute that we could not meet at the George R. Brown Convention Center, canceling the event for an estimated 6,000 attendees. With nowhere to meet, the RPT Chairman held the convention via Zoom. It was the worst experience ever! The joke among the delegates was "We are at ease" because he flashed that message across our screens endlessly for most of the convention.

With the help of the Senate Republican Executive Committee (SREC) members, some of the delegates gathered by senate district in a centralized location to see if we could get any business done. Because I was a delegate from Denton County, my assigned location was Little Elm High School. We gathered at the high school on the convention's first day, only to discover their Wi-Fi was not working.

Faced with a huge dilemma, I offered our SREC member my church for our meeting. We had excellent Wi-Fi, and I was happy to let everyone use it. She agreed, and we met at the church at 11:00 a.m. the next day and resumed the convention.

The most important part of the convention was electing a new chairman. We knew that the party needed new leadership and that Allen West was the solution. When it came time to vote for the new chairman, most of the Frisco Conservatives precinct chairs voted for Allen. I'll never forget staying up into the wee hours of the morning waiting for the results from all thirty-one senatorial districts. When I found out that Allen had won, I was ecstatic! I texted him immediately and congratulated him. I felt he represented a new direction for the party and a changing of the guard for Texas.

Fueled by Allen's win, our PAC's next big assignment was hosting the "We Are the Storm Rally." This event occurred on August 4th, only a few weeks after the convention, to celebrate Allen's success. This was the first "official" rally, debuting him as the party's new chairman.

The event was packed. We must have had around 300 people there. The atmosphere was electric. It felt like people hung on his every word. His message "We Are the Storm" came from a famous quote where the devil whispers to the warrior, "You cannot withstand the storm." The warrior responds, "I am the storm."

I'll never forget what Allen said that day. He looked at the audience and said that Collin County, Denton County, and Tarrant County were the thin red line for Texas. He said that if Trump lost those counties, he would lose Texas. Allen's words went all over me. They weren't just hype or some rah-rah victory speech. They were truth!

I heard the Lord speaking to me at that moment, and I knew we had to hold the line for President Trump. These words cemented our marching orders for our next big assignment.

—

Chapter 5

Cooking with Gas

Frisco Conservatives caught fire after Allen West's rally. His speech inspired us to hold the line for Donald Trump. The first thing we did was to identify fifty-two Republican candidates running for office and make door hangers.

The door hangers were titled "Liberty is on the Line This November" and featured a picture of the Statue of Liberty on the front. On the back, we listed Donald Trump and the other fifty-one Republican candidates we had selected, followed by the message "Don't Stop at the Top. From the White House to the Courthouse Vote Republican on November 3rd."

Our marketing strategy was directed at the 15,000 Republican voters who only voted in presidential elections to encourage them to vote down the ballot. State law had changed straight-party voting in Texas, so we knew the only way to elect our candidates was to encourage down-ballot voting.

We identified three significant advantages over our opponents in the 2020 election. First was Donald Trump. Trump fever was everywhere. Trump convoys were huge at the time, and we participated in all of them. We attended several Trump rallies held in Frisco and joined the long line of Trump supporters driving in the convoys. We also block walked like crazy. My city council campaign taught me that block walking was the key to success. During this election, we distributed Trump yard signs and hung door hangers on over 30,000 doors.

Our second advantage over our opponents was that the May municipal election had been postponed to November due to COVID-19. This was the saving grace for our local candidates. We knew our candidates weren't strong enough to win in a regular municipal election. They needed the 15,000 Republican voters coming out to vote for Trump. We knew we could beat the cabal by running our local candidates alongside our county, state, and federal candidates. We just had to figure out how to encourage our targeted voters to remain at the polls long enough to vote down the ballot.

God gave us another witty idea to overcome this obstacle. Historically, poll greeters who worked in Frisco elections were always unpaid volunteers. No one had ever heard of paid volunteers. Knowing that Christmas was right around the corner and that people might enjoy some extra spending money, we advertised that we were looking for volunteers to poll greet for $10 per hour. News spread fast, and people came out of the woodwork! They were already excited about Trump, so motivating them wasn't hard. The pay was just the cherry on top. Some even worked for free.

We became the first PAC in Frisco to launch the idea of paid volunteers. Our strategy was so successful that we recruited 175 volunteers who helped us poll greet 1,600 hours during early voting and Election Day.

Maybe I'm making this sound easy, but you must understand this was no small feat. Governor Abbott had extended early voting by one extra week, so we didn't just have to cover the customary two weeks of early voting; we had to cover three weeks plus Election Day. We also had to ensure that we had no break in coverage at each of the twenty-four polling locations in Frisco.

Polls were open twelve hours daily, and volunteers were required to work four-hour shifts. This took a tremendous amount of planning on our end. We had to set up and tear down our gear at each location daily. This included tents, tables, chairs, push cards, coolers, snacks, water, and signage. We also had to arrive way before polls opened at 7 a.m. to ensure we got the best spot.

The Lord gave us another witty idea for accomplishing this task. We divided Frisco into four quadrants and assigned captains to oversee each quadrant. The captains were responsible for supervising their polling locations, ensuring they had the supplies they needed, and managing their volunteers. This plan worked so well that we rarely had a break in poll coverage.

The third advantage we had over our opponents was the element of surprise. The cabal had no idea that we were coming. They didn't know our strategy because we wouldn't let them attend our meetings. We had a strict check-in policy and a well-oiled welcome team. If a cabal member showed up to our meeting, we would bounce them at the door.

I'll never forget the night when several of our Frisco school board trustees showed up. They weren't there for benevolent purposes; they showed up for intel. We turned them away at the door and told them they couldn't enter. They were stunned! They couldn't believe we would tell elected officials they weren't welcome at our meetings.

Well, we didn't care. They weren't welcome and we didn't apologize for it. We did not allow elected officials into our meetings unless we held a town hall meeting or candidate forum. This became our policy until the election was over. Keeping our strategy a secret (though very hard to do) was another key to our success.

God also gave us a witty idea regarding communication. WhatsApp was very popular among our members, so we created different

WhatsApp groups to communicate with our volunteers.

Our ability to communicate using this app became one of our greatest assets. It allowed our volunteers to chat about what they were seeing, hearing, and experiencing at the polls. It helped us identify where we were weak and where the opposition was strong.

One of our favorite tactics was sending disrupters to the polls whenever the cabal showed up. Because their team wasn't as large as ours, they had to pick and choose which polling locations they worked. When one of them would show up to talk to voters, someone would chat it in WhatsApp. Our assigned disrupters would see the message and head to that polling location to interfere with the opponent.

We were generally very good at getting there within ten to fifteen minutes. Once our disrupters arrived, they would stand next to the cabal member and irritate them by making their presence loudly known. They would talk to the voters at the same time the cabal did and counter-argue what the cabal member was saying. Spreading the truth about how the cabal ran our city would generally turn their votes toward our candidates.

Another key to our success was that we always tried to be the last person the voters talked to before they headed into the polls. Our volunteers ensured each voter had our push card and were educated on voting down the ballot. My favorite part of our plan was watching the voters who already had our push card when they got out of their car. Some had a copy of our door hanger, and others had downloaded an electronic version from our website. It was so satisfying knowing that we had already reached these voters.

Our push cards were so effective that poll workers told voters they were illegal and couldn't be used inside the polling location. Of course, this wasn't true. They were just mad that our team was winning and theirs was losing. We eventually told voters to fold them up, put them in their pockets, and not take them out until they entered the voting booth.

In the end, it was a blood bath for the opposition. The 2020 election was the largest in Frisco's history, with over 90,000 voters (a 78.15% voter turnout). We not only reached the 15,000 Republican voters we needed, but we got an additional 35,000 we didn't need. All totaled, we handed out 80,000 push cards.

We raised over $100,000 for the election, and 94% of our candidates won their races. We also got our first conservative candidate elected to the city council after beating six opponents in the primary and helping him get across the finish line in the runoff.

We had taken Allen West, seriously. We held the thin-red line in Collin and Denton counties, and Donald Trump won Texas.

As part of our victory celebration, we held a winter gala the following month at a country club in

Frisco. We were honored to host Dinesh D'Souza as our guest speaker. The room was packed with Trump-loving patriots and ardent grassroots volunteers. It looked like an army!

As I gave awards to our top volunteers that evening, what we had accomplished finally sunk in. I realized that we had just done the impossible. The idea that started with twelve of us sitting around a table licking our wounds had become a reality. With just a small contingent of tired, irate patriots, we had fought back and won.

WE BEAT THE CABAL!

Looking back on it now, I realize that unity was our superpower. Our opponents couldn't beat us because we were unified. We didn't all think the same, but we had one goal: to defeat the cabal.

This singular goal helped us look past our differences and focus on what we had in common. We adopted the Ronald Reagan rule early in our PAC's formation. He said, "The person who agrees with you 80 percent of the time is a friend and ally — not a 20 percent traitor."[1]

We lived by that rule, keeping our members focused on the 80 percent that united us, not the 20 percent that divided us. The results were phenomenal!

After our victory, people began recognizing us as a force to reckon with. Our membership doubled in size, and by the end of 2020, we had around 6,000 people following us on social media. This was far more than any of the cabal members had following them. We were cooking with gas!

However, we didn't get to celebrate for long. The Democrats had stolen the election, and there would be heck to pay. Donald Trump's loss left us with a divided party, and Frisco Conservatives was no exception.

Chapter 6

Divided We Fall

Donald Trump's loss was devastating to conservatives nationwide. The Sunday after the January 6th insurrection, I stood before my congregation and told them that God had different plans. I said that we had an executive order—not from Congress or D.C., but from the desk of the CEO of heaven. God's will was that Donald Trump would be president for eight years. I based this mainly on Kim Clement's prophecy about Trump's two presidential terms.

In 2007, Kim prophesied,

> "'This that shall take place shall be the most unusual thing, a transfiguration, a going into the marketplace, if you wish, into the news media, where *Time Magazine* will have no choice but to say what I want them to say. *Newsweek*, what I want to say. *The View*, what I want to say. Trump shall become a trumpet,' says the Lord. 'Trump shall become a

trumpet. I will raise up the Trump to become a trumpet and Bill Gates to open up the gate of a financial realm for the church,' says the Lord.

"For God said, 'I will not forget 9/11. I will not forget what took place that day, and I will not forget the gatekeeper that watched over New York, who will once again stand and watch over this nation,' says the Spirit of God. 'It shall come to pass that the man that I place in the highest office shall go in whispering My name.' But God said, 'When he enters into the office he will be shouting out by the power of the Spirit, for I shall fill him with My Spirit when he goes into office and there will be a praying man in the highest seat in your land. There will be a praying president, not a religious one, for I will fool the people,' says the Lord. 'I will fool the people; yes, I will.' God says, 'The one that is chosen shall go in, and they shall say he has hot blood.' For the Spirit of God says, 'Yes, he may have hot blood, but he will bring the walls of protection on the country in a greater way, and the economy of this country shall change rapidly,' says the Lord of hosts. Listen to the word of the Lord. God says, 'I will put at your helm for two terms a president that will pray, but he will not be a praying president when he starts. I will put him in office, and then I will baptize him with the Holy Spirit and my power,' says the Lord of hosts."[1]

In another prophecy Kim gave in 2007, he said,

"Now, God says, 'A president that I will bring into the White House, and they will say he is ungodly; he does not know God. But even as Jesus disguised himself for the great feast, so I have disguised this man's heart, and when he comes to the White House, not only shall he be Mine, that he shall pray as a man that has never prayed in the White House. That same man, that same man,' says the Spirit of God, 'shall put his feet onto this platform, and,' God says, 'they will say how did this take place?'

"Laws shall change. Young men and young women shall have access into the kingdom, and with authority into politics, and with authority into the industries that now have been controlled by darkness because of this man that shall rule for another two terms. For two terms. God said, 'Do not fear, for the Lord says there will be no unnecessary, unnecessary stuff. But there will be things that man shall question. Fear not for you shall sit in that seat. And suddenly My Spirit shall come upon him and baptize him with fire and with anointing,' says the Spirit of the Lord."[2]

I knew Kim Clement to be a legit man of God. I had attended one of his meetings in California and

---

91

saw firsthand that he was an accurate prophet. His prophecy about Trump sat well in my spirit. I knew that Trump was God's pick for president, and He wanted him to return to the White House.

Many national voices in Christendom echoed this same sentiment during the 2020 election. So, when I stood in front of my congregation on January 10th, I knew what I was saying was by the Spirit of the Lord.

That morning, I led my church in a Jericho march around our sanctuary as we waved American flags and declared that the walls of Jericho would fall. At the end of the service, I discussed the need to prepare for a national blackout or any emergency that could occur between then and inauguration day. I told my congregation to stock up on food, water, and gas generators and to keep their weapons loaded. After January 6th, I wasn't sure what events would unfold next. As a pastor, I wanted my congregation to be safe by being prepared.

My message was being live-streamed that morning, as it is every Sunday. The only difference this Sunday is that it went viral, and the media picked it up. The Wednesday following that service, *The Dallas Morning News* printed an article titled *Frisco Pastor urges followers to keep guns loaded, stock up on food and water before Biden inauguration.*[3]

The article began, "Days after President Donald Trump incited supporters to attack the U.S. Capitol in an effort to overturn the election, an evangelical pastor in Frisco told his congregation they have an 'executive order' to keep Trump in office." The article stated that I cited prophetic voices who said that Trump would be president for eight years and that it was our responsibility, as Christians, to execute God's order. I knew, of course, that I was calling for the ekklesia to pray and issue decrees over the situation. However, the article implied that I was calling for insurrection.

The newspaper didn't stop after one article. A week later, another article came out titled *Frisco pastor's dangerous words, far-right views don't reflect their city, conservative leaders say.*[4]

The article began, "After a Frisco pastor made national headlines for his statements during a Sunday service just days after insurrectionists stormed the U.S. Capitol, city leaders denounced his comments, and several residents expressed fears that Christian nationalism has infiltrated their community." The article quoted one of our Frisco city councilmembers as saying that, "despite self-identifying as one of the most conservative council members, the views of Burden . . . do not align with his, or even most of Frisco's views." Residents were quoted as saying that I had become a safety issue for the community, and they urged the city council to denounce my church publicly.

The persecution grew worse. The day before the first article came out, the PAC hosted an event called

—

The Secrets Behind Black Lives Matter (BLM). I received an influx of phone calls and voicemails over this event, mainly from those within the BLM community. They threatened to show up in droves and stop my meeting. They threatened to destroy my building. One pastor called and yelled at me for so long that I finally just hung up the phone.

The church phone was ablaze with opposition, as evidenced by the eighty-eight voicemails spewing hatred toward us for hosting the event. The pushback was so bad that I was forced to hire private security to conduct the meeting. One of the officers stood in my front lobby with an AR-15 strapped to his shoulder for our protection. The Frisco Police Department and Texas State Troopers also parked their vehicles in my parking lot as a deterrent.

Attendees had to be wanded by security to get in the front door. It was unbelievable! I had never seen anything like it in Frisco. Fortunately, no violence occurred, and we held the meeting as planned. However, the blowback from this meeting and the news article the next day created a wave of persecution that was only the beginning.

Just when I thought the wave of persecution was over I was hit from another angle. The PAC's Board of Directors called a special meeting to discuss my removal as chairman. At the time, our board was mainly comprised of deep pockets, not principled conservatives. Board seats were earned by donating

$1,000 to the PAC. No other qualifications were required. This resulted in an enormous board — seventeen members, to be exact. A lot of these board members were wealthy business owners.

The meeting was called because they felt that my rhetoric hurt their reputation and their businesses in the community. My Vice Chair was concerned that I was a loon because I cited prophetic voices in my message. He said it made me look crazy to the community. Other board members were concerned I was hurting the PAC's reputation by making the Republican Party look bad.

The discussion finally came down to a vote on whether to remove me. Eight voted to remove me and eight voted to keep me. I was the seventeenth vote, and I opted to stay. Six of those eight members resigned the next day. Several more left in the following weeks.

The Dallas Morning News had a heyday with my attempted removal as chairman. They printed another article titled *Frisco pastor temporarily out as chairman of conservative PAC after his comments on Trump, guns.*[5] This article spread like wildfire. Its circulation was not just limited to Dallas; these articles were being syndicated nationwide and in Canada. *Newsweek* picked it up. *The Sacramento Bee* and the *Miami Herald* published it as well. People also made videos about the articles on YouTube. If you Google *Frisco Pastor Trump*, you can still find them.

—

After recognizing that the press wasn't going away, I had to decide how to respond. I knew that an interview with the paper was out of the question. Cancel culture was rampant in our country, and I was a target. If I decided to give an interview or a written statement, I knew that the paper would twist it somehow or not print it accurately. A friend, who was a political consultant, told me I needed to prepare a written statement and put it out on video.

I took his advice, and on January 25th, I finally released a video statement to the community.[6] I told viewers I had become a target of cancel culture and that the establishment media was coming after me. I said that people of faith were under attack in our nation and that, sadly, we would see many more episodes like it.

I also noted that it was unfortunate that some of my words had caused people pain and that I sought the Lord's help in communicating more clearly in the future. I forgave those who had betrayed me and thanked those who supported me. I concluded by saying that I would never back down from the Judeo-Christian beliefs at the core of the American concept and would continue fighting for conservative values.

My video finally quelled the vitriol that was spewing against me. The voicemails died down. Hate letters stopped coming in the mail, and my inbox finally calmed down, too.

The Dallas Morning News printed their fifth and final article on Feb 23rd titled *Frisco pastor promotes false claims of stolen election with event at his church this week.*[7] The article had to do with bringing in Paul Davis, a North Texas attorney fired from his job for attending the January 6th rally at the Capitol. Paul was another patriot who had been targeted by cancel culture. He never went into the Capitol, but was fired for making a video about the rally and posting it on social media.

Paul was famous for filing a lawsuit against the government alleging voter fraud. If successful, it would have possibly triggered a new election. I brought him in on February 24th to discuss how the election was stolen. The meeting was standing room only. People were eager to hear what had gone wrong with the election and what we could do about it.

The remainder of 2021 was a challenge for me. It felt a lot like the months following my campaign. Things didn't seem to go my way. As I said at the beginning of this chapter, Donald Trump's loss devastated all conservatives nationwide, including Frisco Conservatives. The remaining members of our board met to figure out how to keep our PAC together as we reeled from the bad press.

To make matters worse, some of the board members who defected went down the road and started a new PAC. They took a copy of our membership directory and recruited our members to come over to their new group. In one way it was devastating to our membership, but in another, it was a blessing. I figured that anyone who didn't have the courage to stick by our side during troubling times didn't deserve to be a member of our PAC. I wanted warriors by my side, not chickens.

My church also did not escape the persecution of the media attacks. In 2020, we hosted a Christians and Government Workshop with Rev. Rafael Cruz and several other Christian leaders. One of the attendees at this workshop was a self-avowed atheist who sat in the audience and secretly video-recorded the seminar. Later, she and her husband (also a devout atheist) made a video exposing us as Christian Nationalists. The left defines Christian Nationalists as those trying to make America a Christian nation.[8]

I didn't know it then, but this couple contacted the Internal Revenue Service (IRS), asking them to inquire into our 501(c)3 status. Their allegations were that we were crossing the line of separation between church and state by hosting political events at our church, and they accused us of violating the Johnson Amendment. Oh, the dreaded Johnson Amendment (more on that subject in a later book)!

The IRS opened an investigation on us, citing several events we held at the church with prominent

—

black conservative leaders who didn't fit the woke narrative. Their investigation took almost a year.

After the investigation stalemated due to lack of evidence, we finally invited the IRS to visit our property and let them see the church for themselves. They accepted our invitation and sent five agents from five different states to meet with us onsite. After spending a day at our facility, they determined that we had not violated the Johnson Amendment. However, to put their minds at ease, we changed our building policy to no longer allow PACs to use the facility. They accepted the terms and it settled the matter.

This decision unfortunately left Frisco Conservatives without a home. We had been renting the building for our monthly meetings and now we were displaced. After we moved out, our membership numbers took a hit, and our PAC went on life support immediately.

We didn't think our PAC would make it into the new year, so we decided to go out with a bang. We invited U.S. Representative Marjorie Taylor Greene in for a winter gala in December. This kicked off a whole new controversy filled with political fireworks (like I needed another one!). We came under tremendous fire in the community for bringing her in.

One group called "Be the Change" took out a digital billboard on Central Expressway saying,

"Marjorie Taylor Greene, NO THANKS – Frisco Voters."[9] We rented a hotel in Frisco because we couldn't use the church. To the hotel's surprise, they started receiving threatening phone calls stating that protestors planned to show up to shut down our event. Others called, threatening to boycott the hotel if they went through with the meeting.

Local law enforcement was brought in to meet with our paid security team to develop a safety plan. Mall security and hotel security were included, along with Marjorie's private security team. Police cruisers were parked outside with officers inside the hotel to prevent protestors. It started to look like the BLM event all over again.

Fortunately, no protestors showed up, and the event went as planned. We had an extraordinary night with Marjorie as she told the insider story of what was happening in D.C. I especially loved the stories she shared about Nancy Pelosi and Alexandria Ocasio-Cortez.

I'll never forget my chairman's remarks at the gala that night. I stood up and told the crowd that we were going to stop sending politicians down to Austin and to D.C. and that we were going to start sending statesmen. I said emphatically, "We need statesmen—men and women who stand on principle and principle alone. Men and women who don't care if they are popular or can get re-elected. Men and women willing to fight for this nation's moral fabric and stand up for truth in the face of adversity. It is time for cowards to stay home. Let somebody else do the job. If you've got the guts to go up against Nancy Pelosi and Alexandria Ocasio-Cortez like Marjorie Taylor Greene sitting right here, then maybe you are qualified for the job. You may be qualified for the job if you've got the guts to challenge the Jan 6th commission and get our men and women out of prison. If you are willing to go down to Austin and stop playing in the good ole boys club and talking trash about the voters back home, then maybe you are qualified for the job. But if you are unwilling to put principle above popularity, honor above ego, and moral absolutes above political correctness, then maybe you should do us all a favor and stay home."

My words hit hard. One of our state representatives sitting a few rows in front of me turned beet red. He knew that I was talking to him. If only he knew how serious I was about making my promises become a reality that spring. Frisco Conservatives was about to be re-born!

Chapter 7

Austin, Here We Come!

In 2022, we shifted gears and adopted a new mission. After Biden was sworn in as president, we were done with the Republicans in Name Only (RINOs) who refused to stand up for President Trump. We knew the RINOs in the Texas House wouldn't do the right thing without WE, THE PEOPLE, holding them accountable. I had heard one too many stories about their backroom deals and their frequent dinners where they ridiculed the voters back home as they gave each other high fives and declared that in Austin, they did things *their* way.

The first step in our PAC's rebirth was to elect a new board and change our name to North Texas Conservatives. This name better reflected our members and more fully defined our new direction. We set a new mission for ourselves, stating that we existed to educate and advocate for conservative values in the Texas Legislature. Our vision was a pro-conservative Texas that followed the U.S. Constitution as envisioned by our founding fathers.

In the first meeting conducted under our new name, we declared that our main goal was to show up in Austin and hold our representatives accountable. The audience loved it! Everyone was sick of the RINOs, and they expressed it loudly through their cheers.

I had witnessed the power of grassroots lobbying in the previous two legislative sessions. You might recall from Chapter 4 how my testimony in front of the Senate Committee on Property Tax in the 86th Legislature made an impact. The Texas Property Tax Reform and Transparency Act was the result.

I also witnessed the power of the grassroots in the 87th Legislature when I went with the Collin County Republican Party on a chartered bus to lobby for conservative legislation in that session. I'll never forget it. The date was April 29, 2021. HB 1927, the open carry gun bill, was being heard in committee that day. Senator Drew Springer, one of the bill's co-sponsors, stepped out of the committee hearing to meet with us for a few minutes. I was so enthralled that a senator would take time out of his busy schedule to meet with his constituents.

This concept was new to me. I hadn't done any lobbying in Austin except for my singular testimony in 2019. After a successful meeting with Senator Springer and other lawmakers that afternoon, we returned to the bus and headed home. While driving on Interstate 35, we received the news that the open carry bill had been passed out of committee.

Shouts of joy rang out on the bus. It was an absolute high, one that has stuck with me to this day. Right then and there, I understood the power of grassroots lobbying. This trip planted the seed that North Texas Conservatives needed for our success in the 88th Legislature.

After changing our PAC's name and mission, we held monthly roundtables to determine our top ten priorities. These roundtables were wildly popular, as evidenced by the high monthly attendance. People were excited that a group was willing to hold lawmakers accountable.

These meetings were think tank sessions where we allowed people to voice their ideas and strategies for making the 88th Legislature a pro-conservative session. One of our top concerns was voter fraud, as evidenced in the 2020 election. Other concerns included protecting our children, educational freedom, parental rights, securing our border, banning Democrat chairs, medical freedom, defending gun rights, banning Environmental and Social Governance (ESG), abolishing abortion, and fixing the electric grid.

At each roundtable, we would list one of our top ten priorities and then whiteboard ideas for crafting an ideal piece of legislation. These ideas became our talking points for speaking with legislators in Austin.

Although we had a working framework for what we wanted to address with our legislators, we weren't sure how to get in front of them. God had to build my faith for that step, and He used a lady by the name of Evelyn Brooks to do it.

In May 2021, Evelyn ran for the Frisco school board and lost to the cabal. She was a very outspoken candidate who did not shy away from her Christian faith in the classroom. She spoke confidently in the candidate forums and received a standing ovation at the forum our PAC hosted. However, on Election Day, she lost. It was a hard loss for conservatives, especially after the overwhelming defeat we delivered the cabal in the 2020 election.

I didn't see Evelyn again until the fall of 2021, when she became a literature teacher in our homeschool academy. One day, right before the Christmas break, I caught her in the hallway at school and she said, "Pastor, I want to ask you a question."

I said, "Sure."

Wanting my opinion, she asked, "What do you think about me running for the Texas State Board of Education? My husband and I are praying about my run, and I must submit my application next week."

Her question caught me entirely off guard. She had just lost her school board race seven months prior, and that was just a citywide race. Now, she wanted to run for a seat across nineteen counties with a population of 1.9 million. Worse yet, she only had three months until the primary.

I responded to her question with a very religious answer, saying something like, "Well, you know, Evelyn, if God is in it, He will make a way. You know that, with God, all things are possible."

I didn't tell Evelyn what I was really thinking, which was *Evelyn, there's no way in the world you can win in three months. You just lost your school board race and want to run for a state board? You're out of your ever-loving mind! I know what it takes to run a campaign. You know what it takes to run a campaign. We both ran a campaign and lost. How in the world do you think you're going to win?* Thank God I didn't speak what I was thinking out loud.

I didn't see Evelyn for the next three months. Quite honestly, I didn't think much more about our conversation, or pay any attention to whether she filed in December, or not. On March 2nd, the day after her race, I looked at the election results for the primary. Astonishingly, as I skimmed down the page, I saw her name. I couldn't believe it! She had indeed filed. Then I saw the results. She had beat the incumbent 57.2% to 42.8%! *What? This can't be right,* I thought to myself.

Wanting to get to the bottom of it, I picked up the phone and called her. When she answered, I said, "Evelyn, I can't be seeing these results correctly. It says that you just won the primary for the State Board of Education!"

"I know, Pastor! All I can say is God!"

———

107

Astonished, I replied, "Evelyn, tell me how you did it."

She then explained how God provided every step of the way and did miracles that got her across the finish line. She said the Lord laid it upon some momma bears' hearts to get behind her campaign. Even though they had never met her, God put it on their hearts to help her. They started sending out their own mailers, spreading the word about her candidacy like wildfire.

Evelyn said, "Pastor, I didn't have the money. I told my campaign staff we would only spend what God brought in. We didn't have funds to reach nineteen counties, but God did it another way. It was just all God."

I was on the floor by this point, saying to the Lord, "God, this just doesn't happen! You don't win elections this way!"

God replied, "Son, what I did for Evelyn, I will do for you."

I broke down and began to cry as I recognized the voice of my Father. I knew He was speaking to me regarding our assignment in Austin. I didn't know how God would do it, but I believed that if He could do it for Evelyn, He could do it for me.

The board then set a Big, Hairy, Audacious Goal (BHAG®) for making our vision a reality. BHAG® is a concept first developed by business consultant Jim

Collins and American organizational theorist Jerry Porras in the book *Built To Last: Successful Habits of Visionary Companies*. The BHAG® replaces the more traditional mission-driven five-year business plan with a longer-term plan that reaches into the future.

We told the members of our PAC that our BHAG® was to go to Austin every week the legislature was in session and lobby for our priorities. Our job was to charter the buses; their job was to get on the bus. I leveraged the idea of buses from the successful Collin County trip in the 87th session. I knew more people would go with us if we made the trip as convenient as possible by providing transportation.

To make it easy for people, we set up an online Sign-Up Genius, where they could simultaneously reserve seats and pay for their tickets. They could also reserve multiple seats if they wanted to bring others with them. We even gave our BHAG® a name. We called it the "Here Comes the Convoy" bus trips.

We made t-shirts with the state of Texas and a Humvee superimposed over the image with the words "Here Comes the Convoy" on the front and our PAC logo on the sleeve. We wore these shirts proudly as we held our lawmakers accountable each week.

One thing I noticed about Austin during my trip in the 87th session is that lawmakers listened to lobbyists. Whoever bent their ear the last and the hardest would generally get the vote they wanted.

Another thing I learned is that lobbyists were paid to be there every week, whereas the grassroots usually went down only once or twice during the session. This helped me understand that, in Austin, the squeaky wheel got the grease.

I informed our members that we would only be successful if we went to Austin every week; once or twice was not going to cut it. I also recognized that the grassroots movement was the largest lobby in Texas; however, we weren't organized, funded, or consistent. This insight became our golden opportunity.

At first, money was an obstacle to accomplishing our mission because our grassroots lobbyists had to pay their way. The cost to ride the bus roundtrip was $50, and with the hyperinflation of 2023, this amount was cost-prohibitive for some. However, by the middle of the session, generous donors heard what we were doing and began to sponsor the buses for us. These sponsorships allowed us to take 600 people to Austin during the five-month session.

We created a weekly bus schedule for our trips. Recognizing that our members would have more buy-in if they were interested in the topic, we set different themes for each trip. This strategy proved instrumental in rallying the troops. We also had to figure out how to create momentum because we recognized that we didn't have enough members to fill a weekly busload to Austin. This is when God gave us the idea of having leaders' dinners.

We sent invitations to the leaders of PACs, Republican clubs, conservative non-profits, and county parties across the metroplex to attend several dinners where we shared our top ten priorities and asked them to weigh in with their thoughts and ideas.

This strategy worked marvelously. It made our trips to the Capitol a team sport. We didn't care who got the glory or the credit in Austin; we just cared about Texas. This attitude made the other leaders feel like they were a part of the mission. The leaders spread the word very quickly about our bus trips, and in no time, we were headed to Austin on our first assignment.

We took our first trip on January 12, 2023, with the mission of Banning Democrat Chairs. The Lord was so faithful to us! We didn't just pack one bus that day. We filled three buses from five counties with one hundred sixty people. We joined up with a thousand other patriots across Texas in sending Speaker Dade Phelan a message that, as the majority party in the House, we didn't want Democrats chairing our committees.

Appointing the minority party to chair committees was a long-standing tradition in the Texas legislature. Some say it began under President Reagan's administration when Republicans took

111

control of the White House, but I am not sure. All I know is that it had been going on for decades, resulting in weak, watered-down legislation that did not reflect conservative values.

Phelan had appointed thirteen Democratic chairs out of thirty-four standing committees in the 87th session.[1] The following year, delegates at the Texas State Convention responded by passing a priority to ban Democrat chairs in the 88th session.[2] As fellow Republicans, we wanted Speaker Phelan to abide by the party's wishes.

When word spread that the grassroots were coming to Austin to lobby against Democrat chairs, Phelan changed the weekly schedule and released his committee selections the day before our arrival. He reduced the number of Democrat chairs from thirteen to eight (which was an improvement), but we were steamed that he didn't allow us to show up on the day the vote was taken so we could make our voices heard. We knew he was snubbing his nose at us, saying he was in charge.

We responded by showing up in our red "Ban Democrat Chairs" t-shirts the next day and packing out the House gallery. We made our presence and feelings loudly known. We also sent a message to Dade Phelan in a press conference held outside the Capitol with Republican leaders that afternoon.

Surrounded by a thousand red shirts, Republican leaders condemned Dade Phelan's childish actions and told him we were not going away. We were going to watch his every move, and I'm proud to say that we made good on our promise during the session, as you will read in the following pages.

We took our next trip to Austin on January 24th to lobby for election reform. We worked alongside a group called Texas First which set up a legislative briefing with Senator Bob Hall. In this briefing, Senator Hall laid out his plan for making Texas elections more accurate, transparent, and accountable. Eyewitnesses gave their accounts of voter fraud in Texas, and a panel of cyber experts showed the audience how to hack a voting machine from a cell phone using the voting machine's built-in Bluetooth or USB port. We were shocked that a voting machine didn't have to be connected to a network to be hacked!

Our job on this trip was to visit lawmaker's offices and ask them to watch the briefing on their televisions. We also took them goodie bags with information about voter fraud and how we could fix it. I'll never forget one Republican lawmaker's office I visited. As I stood at the receptionist's desk speaking to one of the staffers about our purpose for being there, the lawmaker stepped out of his office and charged around the corner at me. He got in my face and started hammering me with questions.

"Where's the voter fraud? Where's the proof?" he demanded.

He started getting hot under the collar as I explained how the 2020 election had been stolen. I had seen Dinesh D'Souza's movie *2,000 Mules*, but I wasn't sure he had.

As I expounded on my knowledge, he retorted, "You can't prove that!"

With steam coming out of his ears, he criticized me, and then he said something that stunned me. He said, "What's the problem? We're winning."

My jaw hit the ground. I couldn't believe what I had just heard. A Republican member of the Texas House had just confessed that he knew cheating was happening, but he didn't think it was a big deal so long as Republicans were winning. At that moment, I realized that Democrats weren't the only ones cheating. Republicans were cheating, too.

My eyes were opened as the truth of what was really going on hit me like a ton of bricks. I finally understood why another Republican official in Denton County had refused to allow elected precinct chairs to review ballots that had been cast in the Republican primary. I was beginning to connect the dots as I surmised that corruption was happening on both sides.

The highlight of my trip to the Capitol on January 24th was the prayer rally held on the Capitol steps. The temperature was freezing that day. I was bundled in about five layers of clothing. My good friend, Apostle Bob Long, was there that day, too.

Spending the day at the Capitol with him was such a privilege. He is my long-term mentor and spiritual father. He has extensive experience relating to Christians and the civil government.

As we stood in the crowd, shivering down to our boots, I knew that history was being made. During a prayer assignment at the Capitol a few months prior, the Lord told me that the 88th Legislature would be a double new beginning for Texas. The number eight in Scripture speaks of new beginnings, and I knew the Lord was saying to me that this session would be different. In this session, we were going to see the hand of the Lord move through His outstretched arm.

As a pastor, I was asked to pray something at the rally that afternoon. The Lord laid it upon my heart to pray Clay Nash's *Declaration of Dependence by Patriotic Citizens of the United States of America as Ekklesia E Pluribus Unum*.[3] I opened my mouth and said, "We declare a fresh and renewed dependence upon God our Father, Yeshua our king, and Holy Spirit our co-laborer. We declare a renewed surrender to Robert Hunt's 1607 prayer of covenant:

'We do hereby dedicate this land, and ourselves, to reach the people within these shores with the gospel of Jesus Christ, and to raise up godly generations after us, and with these generations take the kingdom of God to all the earth. May this *Covenant of Dedication* remain to all generations, as long as this earth remains, and may this land, along with England, be evangelist to the world. May all who see this cross, remember what we have done here, and may those who come here to inhabit join us in this covenant and in this most noble work that the Holy Scriptures may be fulfilled.'"

I could feel the anointing of the Holy Spirit pulsating through my veins as I declared these words. My body was electrified by the time I got to the last statement, "As a follower of Yeshua, we vow our dependence upon God's guidance totally. We declare that America shall be saved and preserved by faith, repentance, mercy, unity, reverence, and dependence on our Supreme God Almighty."

I knew in my spirit that I was decreeing a shift over the legislature that would result in a new beginning for the State of Texas. The 88th Legislature was not going to be business as usual.

Our next trip to Austin didn't occur until March. Hardly anything goes on in the legislature during February. Lawmakers can file bills during the first sixty calendar days of the session, but committees aren't allowed to start receiving public testimony until March. Then, it is a mad scramble to get bills passed in less than ninety days. I'm not sure who created this system, but I would love to give them a piece of my mind. Some say this system is effective because it forces us to do all of our state's business quickly. However, it is also designed to run the clock out and kill a lot of good legislation that should be passed (that's a discussion for another time).

For those of you who are unfamiliar with the legislative process in Texas, we hold our legislative sessions once every two years. The regular session starts in early January and has a hard stop at the end of May. Our state can also hold special sessions for any unfinished business during the regular session, but only the governor can call those sessions.

The reason why it is so important to go to Austin and lobby during the regular session is because our state is forced to do all of its business for the next two years during that short window. All of the bills that are going to fail or be passed into law are determined during that timeframe.

The agenda of each session is driven by the bills that the lawmakers file. Bills that make it into committee have a chance for public input, which is generally the most important part of the proposed bill's life cycle. If a bill makes it out of committee, it can be placed into the Calendars Committee to see if it will ever reach the House floor. Once it reaches the floor, it can be amended, killed, or passed. The bill then has to go to the opposite chamber for passage. Once both chambers pass the same version of the bill, it can then go to the governor's desk to be signed into law.

Grassroots involvement in the legislative process, when done proficiently, can determine what becomes law in our state. This is why our efforts in the 88th Legislature were so important.

Starting in March, we went to the Capitol every week as promised.

- March 7th, we participated in Texas Education Day by lobbying for a bill that would remove pornographic books from Texas public school libraries.

- March 14th, we focused on securing the Texas border.

- March 21st, we advocated for parental rights and educational freedom by testifying in front of the public education committee in favor of HB 900.

- March 28th, we lobbied for banning Environmental and Social Governance (ESG), a social credit system that allows governments like China to take away citizens' freedom.

- April 4th, we focused on fixing the Texas electric grid to prevent outages like we had during snowmaggedon in 2021.

- April 11th, we fought for medical freedom by resisting the tyranny of forced masking and vaccinations by companies.

- April 20th, we pushed for a ban on child gender

modification by hosting a briefing with detransition survivors.

- April 25th, we held a Stop Sexualizing Texas Kids Day of Action and Prayer at the Capitol.

- May 2nd, we packed out the House gallery to Save Texas kids by supporting SB 14, the Ban Child Gender Modification Bill.

- May 16th, we held a meeting in the Old Supreme Court Room for Reversing the Kinsey Decision Day. Kinsey was a sicko who conducted research that was used to rewrite the penal code, lessening the penalties for sodomy and pedophilia in all fifty states.

Our most important work during the session was protecting Texas kids. The children of Texas (and honestly, worldwide) are under assault like never before. From human trafficking to sex slavery to gender confusion, I have never seen a time when the devil wants to destroy a generation as badly as he does today. He knows that if he can destroy a generation, he can delay the purpose of God for the next generation.

This is why I believe the Lord sent us to Austin — to destroy the weapons of the devil formed against our kids. Our primary focus in the 88th Legislature was to pass laws that protected our kids from sexualization.

My eyes were opened to this assignment when I attended the Texas Education 911 Day on March 7th. That morning, I participated in a briefing titled Stop Sexualizing Texas Kids. Before the briefing began, Christin Bentley, State Republican Executive Committeewoman (SREC) for Senate District 1, handed me a packet with a cover letter addressed to our state representatives.

Attached to this letter were pages of illustrated images on how to masturbate, use sex toys, and how to research kinks and fantasies. The information included how to perform anal sex, oral sex, homosexual images and where to find pornography online. She explained how these images were in books in Texas public school libraries in all 254 counties in our state. I couldn't believe my ears!

My kids are homeschooled and have never been a part of the public school system. I had heard about pornography in our schools from other parents and grandparents, but had never witnessed it firsthand until that day. I almost fell out of my chair during Christin's presentation. I felt sick to my stomach. Grief immediately swept over me, and I began to mourn inside as I realized what Texas children were being exposed to.

My heart was broken. These kids were under Satan's attack, and something had to be done about it. I went home and immediately spread the word about what was happening to anyone who would listen.

Two weeks later, I was privileged to return to the Capitol to testify before the Public Education Committee on HB 900, known as "The READER Act."[4] The READER Act was a piece of legislation authored by Rep. Jared Patterson to remove sexually explicit materials from public school libraries.

There was much controversy over the bill, mainly over what was considered sexually explicit versus sexually relevant material. The bill's opponents argued that we were acting like Nazis by banning sexually explicit books from school libraries. However, the supporters of the bill argued that we were only removing materials that included a written description, illustration, photographic image, video image, or audio file. We also asked that all library material not directly related to a curriculum (e.g., biology) that described, depicted, or portrayed sexual conduct in a patently offensive way be removed.

Representative Patterson explained that sexually explicit material included items considered indecent by the Federal Communications Commission (FCC) and would never be broadcast on television and radio between 6 a.m. and 10 p.m. when there is a reasonable risk that children may be in the audience.

I couldn't wrap my mind around how books like this ever made it into the school libraries in the first place. If kids couldn't watch it on television, how could they access it at school? It wasn't until I got involved with HB 900 that I learned the issue rested with the book vendors.

Texas did not have a law regulating what books vendors could sell to schools before HB 900. It was the Wild West—any book could be sold to a school. Worse yet, school librarians didn't know what was on their shelves.

Rep. Patterson explained that the district would order thousands of books when a new school was built, and the vendors would stock the shelves for the school before it opened. Sometimes, the school hadn't hired a new librarian yet. When the librarian arrived on their first day, they had no idea what was on the shelves. The school board trustees didn't know either.

Only the book vendors knew what they were stocking the shelves with, and they were very crafty in slipping in these pornographic books. HB 900 changed this by requiring vendors to rate these books as sexually explicit or sexually relevant. Sexually explicit books had to be removed by the vendor, but sexually relevant books could remain.

A sexually relevant book might have to do with a curriculum, such as biology, or a piece of literature, like *A Midsummer Night's Dream* or *The Canterbury Tales*. But sexually explicit books displayed obscene images of pornographic acts.

One of the Public Education Committee members, Rep. James Talarico, tried to kill the bill by arguing the definition of sexually explicit. I sat in the committee hearing the night he argued over whether we could define what sexually explicit meant.

He asked Rep. Patterson, "What's your favorite book?"

"The Bible," he replied.

Talarico responded with, "My favorite book is Lonesome Dove." He then argued whether his book, a literature classic, would be considered sexually explicit under Patterson's definition because it mentioned "poke," a reference to having sex with whores.

Rep. Patterson replied that sexually explicit was defined by whatever the FCC considered indecent. Talarico then asked whether the Bible would be regarded as indecent because it contained stories of incest, like in the story of Lot and his two daughters.

This created an argument that went on for what seemed like endless hours. After a while, I grew tired of listening. After sitting in the committee hearing for the entire day, I wasn't sure if I would ever get to testify.

Finally, my name was called around 10:00 p.m. I had not prepared my testimony ahead of time. I like to base my testimony on what I'm hearing in the room, so I wrote it while sitting there. After listening to Talarico go on and on about the definition of sexually explicit, I directed my comments at him. I said, "Regarding the language in the bill, we can call it obscene, we can call it sexually explicit, we can call it harmful material, we can call it pornography, we can call it whatever we want. The bottom line is that it is wrong and grieves God."

Since Talarico had used the Bible as a reference, I said, "The Bible has a word for it. It is called sin, which means to miss the mark. This practice of allowing these sexually explicit books to remain in our public schools misses the mark. Furthermore, it is child abuse. It steals a child's innocence and breaks down their barriers to sexual encounters, sexual grooming, and sexual abuse. This must be stopped. Our children must be protected."

I figured since Talarico had given us all a Bible lesson that, as a pastor, I should probably give him one, too. I continued, "God created sex as a gift between a man and a woman within the bounds of matrimony, and it was also given as a gift for procreating as we fulfill God's mandate in Genesis 1:28 to be fruitful and multiply and fill the earth. To debase a child's mind and turn the concept of sex into anything else is wrong, immoral, unethical, and outright harmful. God will hold all of us accountable if we do not protect the children of this state. I leave you with one Scripture. Proverbs 14:34 says, 'Righteousness exalts a nation, but sin is a reproach to any people.' Let's roll the reproach off the greatest state in our union. Let's pass HB 900. Thank you."

When I finished, you could hear a pin drop in the room. I was only one of two pastors who testified before the committee that evening. The other pastor had testified regarding the mental damage that pornography causes adolescents. He came at it from a scientific research standpoint. So, I was the only pastor who came at it from a Biblical standpoint.

When I was finished, I went out into the hallway with the other convoy members, and we took a picture together. To our surprise, one of the committee members stepped outside the room to speak to us. He thanked us for coming to testify, and he thanked me, especially for speaking out as a pastor. He said that they didn't get too many pastors showing up in Austin. He was grateful for my testimony and wished more pastors would do the same.

I felt elated that evening, knowing that I had stepped up and done something to protect Texas children. I thought of my kids back home and how, as a father, I had protected them and possibly their kids one day. I drove home excited about what was happening in Austin, but things were about to get rough.

Chapter 8

Prayer at the Capitol

The month of April is when the fireworks began to explode in the state legislature. SB 14, the Ban Child Gender Modification Bill, was the reason for the explosion.

This bill, written by Senator Donna Campbell, M.D., and co-sponsored by Rep. Tom Oliverson, M.D., prohibited healthcare providers from allowing gender-transitioning drugs and gender reassignment surgery to treat gender dysphoria in minors.[1] Gender transitioning had been perpetrated on thousands of teenagers in Texas because no law was in place to stop it. Dr. Campbell and Dr. Oliverson devised a strategy for stopping this practice by writing a piece of legislation that tackled the issue from a medical perspective versus a moral perspective.

By early April, Dr. Campbell's version had been passed in the Senate but had not been taken up by the House. As emotions began to heat up over the bill, I knew it would be a long, drawn-out battle.

Holding onto the promise that the 88th Session would be a double new beginning for Texas, I asked God to intervene, but I knew it wouldn't come without a fight.

On one of my previous trips to the Capitol, trans activists had marched through the hallways inside the extension building, yelling and chanting for their rights. Staffers were forced to lock their office doors, and we were prevented from further lobbying that day. I didn't know then that their antics were just the warmup for what they had planned on May 2nd.

As we entered the month of April, the Lord began to unfold a three-pronged strategy for getting this bill passed. Prong number one involved a Ban Child Gender Mod Day at the Capitol on April 20th. Prong number two involved a Stop Sexualizing Texas Kids Day of Action and Prayer on April 25th. Prong number three involved a massive Save Texas Kids sit-in in the House gallery on May 2nd.

Prong one rolled out on April 20th when we went to Austin to lobby for HB 1686, the companion bill to SB 14, written by Dr. Oliverson. A companion bill is one that is identical to another bill filed in the opposite chamber. By April 20th, Dr. Oliverson's bill had already passed in committee with an amendment that allowed doctors to wean kids currently on puberty blockers so they didn't come off cold turkey. His bill was ready to be placed on the Calendars Committee the day we planned to be at the Capitol.

Our job on that trip was twofold. First, to thank the five authors and seventy-seven co-authors of the bill by performing office visits. Team members made thank you bags to drop off at their offices, and another PAC made thank you cards for us to drop off with the bags. Our second task was to visit the House Calendars Committee and petition that HB 1686 be voted out of committee. Eleven members were on the committee, and the goal was for each team member to fill out green slips in all eleven offices.

Most committee member offices have green slips and red slips. Green slips show the committee member that you support the bill, and red slips show that you oppose the bill. Staff members tally those slips and report the totals to committee members to show how much support or opposition a bill has.

These numbers are extremely important when a committee member is deciding how he or she will vote on a bill. We brought eighty-five people on this trip, which allowed us to break into seventeen teams and quickly knock these office visits out in the morning.

During the afternoon, we attended a briefing with transgender survivors. I was inspired as heroes like Chloe, Prisha, Kevin, and others told their stories of transitioning to the opposite sex and then de-transitioning back to their birth sex. Their testimonies of irreparable damage done to their bodies were horrific. Insurance wouldn't cover their de-transition procedures, and they were kicked to the curb with no one to help them.

I learned that de-transitioners were among one of the fastest-growing communities in society and that nobody wanted them. The LGBTQ community rejected them because they no longer fit the narrative of a homosexual. The straight community also refused them because they didn't fit the narrative of a heterosexual.

One of the speakers, Chloe Cole, testified that she wanted to become a mother. However, she would never be able to breastfeed a child because of her double mastectomy. Even worse, her skin grafts had not healed properly, causing complications from her procedure. Chloe's story was indeed one of bravery. Her inspiring story stoked the fire within my heart to do everything I could to save the children of Texas.

Prong number two was the *Stop Sexualizing Texas Kids Day of Action and Prayer* held on April 25th. Christin Bentley and I planned this event together as an all-out blitz against the powers of darkness holding Texas kids captive.

Several weeks before this event occurred, the Lord began speaking to me in the wee hours of the morning about the historical significance of April 25th. I discovered that April was the month of Nisan on the Jewish calendar, a month that commemorates the Jewish people's miraculous redemption from slavery in Egypt and the birth of the Jewish nation. It is when the Jews observe Passover by removing all leaven from their possession, eating matzah, and telling their children the story of the Exodus.

I also discovered that April was significant on the Gregorian calendar because it was the fourth month of our year. Four is significant in scripture because God created the times and seasons on the fourth day of creation. Prophetically speaking, the number four signifies an appointed time by God. It illustrates God showing up in the natural realm as He did with the fourth man in the fire in the story of Shadrach, Meshach, and Abednego. Four is like God saying, "I'm here, and I'm in your midst. I haven't left or forsaken you, and I'm about to do a miracle that will astonish you."

In addition, I learned that April 25th fell on the eighth month of the other Jewish calendar (the Jewish people have two calendars).[2] Eight has special significance in Scripture as the number for new beginnings. Eight is when God does a new thing in the earth. Eight is when God does a reset. Eight is when God restores what has been lost.

April 25th also fell in the Hebrew year 5783 — a year that signified divine recovery. This brought great courage to my heart as I realized that although saving Texas kids would be an uphill battle, we would recover all.

God also revealed to me the significance of the number twenty-five in scripture. Twenty-five is a

131

number that speaks of double grace to accomplish the mission. It also speaks of God's enabling grace to harvest a crop that's been a long time coming, like dividends after a long investment. Examples of this in scripture include when Jacob received all that was his from his Uncle Laban after twenty long years of labor, and when Israel received their deliverance from the Philistines with the birth of Samson.

God showed me through the number twenty-five that the war over our kids was ending. God was bringing Texas deliverance on April 25th, the same way He brought deliverance to the children of Israel.

As I continued to research the historical significance of April 25th, I came across a story that solidified what God was wanting to show me about this date. Between 1497 and 1504, an Italian explorer named Amerigo Vespucci participated in two voyages to the New World, first on behalf of Spain and then for Portugal.

In 1503 and 1505, two booklets were published under his name, containing colorful descriptions of these explorations and other alleged voyages.

Both publications were widely read across much of Europe because they were popular. Though Cristopher Columbus discovered the New World several years earlier, Vespucci's writings made the New World famous.

In 1507, a German cartographer named Martin Waldseemueller was so inspired by Vespucci's voyages that he created a map of his discoveries. On April 25, 1507, he and his collaborator, Matthias Ringmann, released the published copy of their map, and they named it America, a word derived from a Latinized form of Amerigo's name.

This is the first recorded usage of the word "America" to describe the New World.[3]

I knew I had struck gold. This world history nugget revealed to me that God was intervening in the timeline of America once again. He showed me that He was going back to the root of our nation — to the seed of what became America even before the pilgrims arrived. God was re-seeding the ground of our destiny once again. He was removing the stench of Egypt and the plague of Pharaoh's rule over our land.

It was no mistake that we would be in the Capitol on April 25th. It was no mistake that the theme for that day was "Stop Sexualizing Texas Kids." It was no mistake that the grassroots were advocating for laws that protected children from sexually explicit materials, pornography, and sexually oriented performances in their schools. It was no mistake that a Millstone Package of Bills that would protect our children from sexualization would be passed out of the Calendars Committee during that week. And it was no mistake that pastors, parents, grandparents, and prayer warriors would be gathered from all across our state to lift our voices in prayer that day

133

and say, "No more! Not this generation! Not on our watch! God, come again and rebirth America!"

I was so fired up with this revelation that I could barely sleep that night. My spirit was ablaze with reformation. The next day, I posted a promo video of this newfound revelation, blasting it across every medium available. The results were amazing.

In conjunction with Christin Bentley's leadership in the Republican Party, we gathered 300 people at the Capitol on April 25th. The show of solidarity was overwhelming. We blitzed offices that afternoon with the Millstone Package of Bills. The Millstone Package of Bills is a term coined by Christin. Based on Matthew 18:6, this creative piece of advertising listed all the Millstone bills we were championing to protect Texas kids from sexualization.

The package included bills that prohibited sexually explicit materials in Texas school libraries, protected kids from accessing online pornography, and protected kids from Critical Gender Theory. It included bills that affirmed parental oversight of human sexuality instruction, increased the criminal penalty for sexually grooming children, and repealed the obscenity exemption from the Texas penal code, undoing decades of harm perpetrated by the Kinsey Doctrine.

After dropping the Millstone Package off at lawmakers' offices, we attended a legislative briefing and a meal at 5:30 p.m. Then, at 6:30 p.m., we participated in a worship and prayer service hosted by Rep. Steve Toth in the Capitol extension. That's when the real fireworks began!

Just a little back story here. When the session started in January, Apostle Bob Long asked me if I would lead a night of prayer and worship at the Capitol. He told me I needed to bring in my worship team, and after worship, I was to bring a message and pray. I could pick any Tuesday night; I just had to tell him which one I wanted.

I accepted Bob's invitation and told him I could do the night of April 25th. I confirmed with my brother-in-law, Landon, who leads worship at my church, if April 25th was good for him. He said it was. Mind you, all of this was planned out in January. We had no clue what the session would look like or what obstacles we would face.

This shows you the providence of Almighty God. Our heavenly Father knew that we were supposed to be in the Capitol on that strategic night. With the revelation of the historical significance of April 25th boiling in my spirit and the knowledge that HB 1686 was under attack, I knew that the night of prayer and worship would be anything but ordinary.

First, the attendance was extraordinary. Over two hundred people stayed for prayer that evening, one hundred twenty-six of whom I brought on the buses. Another church brought a busload from Texarkana.

Our crowd was so large they moved us from the fellowship hall into the large auditorium to accommodate us.

Second, the atmosphere was electric. The anointing fell instantly when my brother-in-law hit the first chord on his guitar that evening. I could feel the power and presence of God permeating every square inch of the room. I knew immediately in my spirit that this would be an ekklesia style gathering.

By the time Landon got to the third song, *Let It Rain*, the power of God overtook the room. The atmosphere was completely enveloped in glory.

I took the platform to deliver my message, but knew I wouldn't preach that night. God had a different agenda. He wanted to shift the legislature that evening. The war over HB 1686 was at its peak. The enemy wanted it stopped, but God wanted it passed.

As Landon played instrumentally in the background, I exhorted the crowd. I informed them that we were going to be an ekklesia that evening. I quickly explained that the New Testament Greek Lexicon defined ekklesia as being "an assembly of the people convened at the public place of the council for the purpose of deliberating."[4] In Matthew 16:18, the first recorded usage of this term in scripture, Jesus uses it in the context of the gates of hell not prevailing against the church (ekklesia).

The disciples understood that Jesus was talking about a governmental term because He used it in the context of the Roman ekklesia that ruled over Israel. He was telling His disciples that He was building a spiritual kingdom that would one day govern the world. This is where the early church got their idea of a legislative assembly that turned the world upside down (Acts 17:6).

I taught the people that our job that evening was to legislate some things as God's government on the earth. I told them it wasn't necessary to understand what we were doing entirely. The important thing was that they all agreed that God wanted HB 1686 passed and that the legislature was going to shift into agreement with His will that night.

Without hesitation, the people shouted, "Amen!" I felt such synergy in the room. We had believers from many backgrounds represented, yet it astounded me how unified the people were. We were truly in one place, in one accord, ready for the Holy Spirit to be poured out (Acts 2:1).

As we lifted our voices and began to pray, the power of God came stronger. The roar created by our symphony of prayer sounded like the crashing of many waters. As the worship team continued to play, I could feel the power of God going out of the room and into every office throughout the extension building. I then felt the wind of the Holy Spirit change direction. I knew that God had just blown out the darkness in the Capitol, and the light had come.

137

The Lord then prompted me to come into agreement with the lawmakers in the room. We needed agreement with a civil ruler if the bill was to shift. My eye caught a State Representative from Ft. Worth, an outstanding freshman lawmaker whom I had met on my many journeys to the Capitol. The Lord said, "Pull him up here."

I pulled him up and said, "Mr. Representative, prophesy! Prophesy over this bill." I knew he could prophesy because he was a Christian brother who attended a Spirit-filled church in Ft. Worth, and some of the members from his church had filled me in on his faith.

The Representative quickly shared his story of miraculously being elected to the State House after God instructed him to take his shoes off and walk barefoot seven times around the Capitol like the Israelites did at the Battle of Jericho (Joshua 6:1-27).

After sharing his testimony, he began to prophesy over HB 1686. The ekklesia came around him and agreed and decreed out what he was praying. It was the perfect picture of the ekklesia's role in civil government. After the Representative was done, I knew that the bill had shifted. We had accomplished our mission.

I was one of the last participants to leave the auditorium that night. Walking through the extension building, I headed up the Capitol elevator and exited onto the first floor. As I walked towards the rotunda, I heard singing. As I entered the rotunda, the singing got louder, and I realized it was coming from the convoy. They were singing *Let It Rain* as they posed for a group photo.

Seeing my group worshipping together, I immediately shouted, "Jesus!" and they all clapped and shouted for joy. It was such a powerful moment. A DPS officer came over and silenced us, letting us know that committee hearings were still ongoing, even though it was late at night. We complied, but huddled in the rotunda's center before we left and quietly released our decrees over the main Capitol building.

We declared that all lawmakers in the Capitol building would hear the whisper of God's voice in their offices the next day and that they would do His will regarding HB 1686. One of the ladies in the group saw a powerful beam of light so bright that it broke through the top of the rotunda. It came straight down, hit the Texas seal on the floor, and shook the Capitol building to the point that she felt the ground move beneath her feet. She heard the Lord say that He would shake the Capitol and everyone in it.

She told me that she did not have strong visions often and that she usually didn't tell others until they came to pass. However, she felt the urging of the Holy Spirit to tell me what she saw that night. I confirmed that what she saw was truly from the Lord. As you will read in the next chapter, God was about to shake everything that could be shaken.

We got on the buses and headed for home. It started raining when we got a few miles from the Capitol, and I knew God was smiling on us with His affirmation. His rain had indeed fallen that night as His glory and presence filled every square inch of the Capitol.

Three days later, SB 14, the companion bill to HB 1686, was approved in the Calendars Committee and scheduled for a hearing on the House floor. We now had our horse in the race. The ban on gender modification in Texas was about to become a reality, but it wouldn't come without a fight!

Chapter 9

The Divine Turnaround

Our third prong for protecting Texas children was to pack the House gallery in support of SB 14, the Ban Child Gender Modification Bill. By this point in the session, our buses were being sponsored weekly by generous donors.

People across the state noticed what we were doing, and the money began to roll in like a river. One of our most touching donor stories was from a woman and her husband. When she saw what we were doing on Facebook, she wired us $10,000 to sponsor four buses to Austin. Right after she wired us the money, she let us know that her husband also wanted to send us some money, but he wanted to snail mail it. I, of course, agreed.

I gave her our mailing address and didn't think much more of it. A couple of weeks later, his check arrived in the mail, and it was for $5,000. Super grateful, I sent her a message asking her to thank her husband for me. She informed me that her husband had passed shortly after writing the check. He thought our actions were so wonderful, bold, and courageous that he wanted to contribute to our mission.

I was so deeply moved when I heard this story that I broke down and cried. Even though I wasn't related to this man, I received his gift like an inheritance from a father to a son. I could hear my heavenly Father speaking through his gift, saying, "Keep on going, son. I believe in you." I still get choked up when I tell this story.

On May 2nd, we returned to the Capitol to pack the gallery for SB 14, which is more challenging than it sounds. The gallery seats around five hundred people, but we only brought ninety-three on the buses. The Republican Party wanted a sea of red in the gallery to outshine the protestors gathered in the rotunda. Fortunately, other Republicans from across the state showed up that day, so we filled most of the gallery seats in our red "Save Texas Kids" shirts. The protestors were limited to seating in the back of the room as we filled three sides of the gallery.

We waited six and a half hours for our bill to come up. This was the second scheduled reading of the bill, which was crucial because it was the moment when Dr. Oliverson was allowed to lay out his bill on the House floor and then answer questions from the members. The first reading occurs when the bill is assigned to a committee. The second reading is when most of the significant debate takes place and it is also when most of the amendments are attached by members of the House. These amendments generally water down the bill or sometimes kill it completely. We knew that this bill had to make it through the second reading unscathed if we were to have a strong ban on child gender modification in Texas.

As Dr. Oliverson walked to the podium to lay out his bill, I held on tightly to the word of the Lord. I agreed with what God had said five days earlier during the night of prayer and worship at the Capitol, and I declared in my heart, "This bill shall pass!"

No sooner had Dr. Oliverson opened his mouth than a member rose in opposition to the bill with a point of order. A point of order is a legislative maneuver meant to kill a bill on a technicality. Democrat State Representative Mary González of Clint claimed that the bill cited a study from the *American College of Pediatrics* when the organization is actually called the *American College of Pediatricians*. This one technicality was enough to stop the bill from being read.

Speaker Phelan called Rep. González up to the dais while he tried to work out the problem. A few seconds later, in the ensuing silence, a protest broke out in the gallery. A woman went behind the Speaker's desk and shouted from the balcony, "One, two, three, four, trans folks deserve more." As she continued screaming, others in the back of the room joined in with the chanting. Protestors immediately unfurled two banners over the balcony railing in tandem.

The Speaker came on the microphone, reminding the guests in the audience that outbursts of any kind were not allowed. Nevertheless, the chanting continued.

A few seconds later, the Speaker returned to the microphone and said, "Pursuant to the House constitutional authority to prevent obstruction to these proceedings, the Chair orders the sergeant at arms to clear the gallery. The House will stand at ease until the gallery is cleared."

We were stunned. Quite honestly, we weren't sure what to do at this point. Our group had never experienced a riot at the Capitol before. At first, we remained in our seats. We thought that the DPS officers would only clear out the protestors. After all, they were the ones disrupting the proceedings. However, after a few more seconds, the gallery attendants made it clear that we also had to leave.

Some of our members grew quite upset with these orders. After all, we hadn't caused a scene. We had sat quietly in our seats for six and a half hours, waiting for our bill to be read. Why did we have to be punished?

We finally got up and started to move at the attendants' request.

144

The protestors were obnoxious. One trans protestor lifted his skirt and mooned everybody in the gallery (no, he was not wearing underwear!). Another protestor resisted officers and refused to leave. He was the organizing director with the Texas Freedom Network. He had to be physically restrained and removed by DPS officers. A second protestor was also arrested by officers, but was released on-site. They both faced two misdemeanor charges of disrupting a public meeting and resisting arrest, and a second-degree felony charge for assault on a peace officer.

Sadly, the county attorney's office later rejected the misdemeanors, and a municipal court judge ordered the felony charge be disposed of, according to *The Texas Tribune*.[1] It was total chaos in the House chamber. It looked like a three-ring circus, and I had never seen anything like it.

The worst part of this experience was walking through the two lines of protestors outside the gallery doors. As we filed past them, they shouted at the top of their lungs, "Trans rights are human rights!"

When I got through the two lines of people and turned right to enter the rotunda, a protestor shouted, "You hate me! You hate me!" This protestor rattled me the most because his words bothered me to my core. I couldn't understand why he thought my taking away his right to mutilate himself was hateful. I felt it was true love. It might have been tough love, but I felt it was truly love.

In my heart of hearts, I didn't want this kid and others like him to live a life of misery like de-transitioners Chloe, Prisha, and Kevin. How deceived this kid was not to understand this! I couldn't help but wonder what had happened in his life to make him this way.

We live in such a fatherless generation. I wonder if he had no father, or perhaps an absent or abusive father. I could sense the orphan heart operating through this individual. The orphan heart is a learned behavior that becomes entrenched in the internal paradigm or mind-set of a wounded individual. It most commonly occurs from a deep father wound that scars the soul and separates the child from their God-given identity and purpose.[2]

The *transurrection* at the Capitol (as it came to be called) not only forced us to vacate the gallery, it forced us to evacuate the entire building. All guests and non-essential personnel were forced to leave. It became apparent in the days following the riot that this had all been orchestrated. The protestors knew the only way to stop this bill was to shut the Capitol down. So, that's what they did.

Their behavior was a perfect example of 1 Peter 5:8, "Be alert and of sober mind. Your enemy, the devil, prowls around like a roaring lion looking for someone to devour."

Scripture doesn't say that the enemy is a roaring lion. It says that he acts *like* a roaring lion. My old pastor used to say that he had no teeth because Jesus already kicked them in. All he has left is his voice. Our enemy uses that voice to intimidate and scare us.

These protestors were trying to do just that—scare us away. But it didn't work. We were right back at it three days later.

After the typo was fixed in committee, SB 14 returned to the House floor for another attempted reading on May 5th. Our convoy members returned to the Capitol to support the bill a second time. Democrats, however, killed the bill again on several more points of order. The bill was subsequently sent back to the committee for a second repair. Finally, the bill returned for its third attempted reading on Friday, May 12th.

Once again, our convoy members returned to the Capitol to support the bill. The Democrats immediately tried to kill the bill on two points of order. This time, however, the points were not sustained. Dr. Oliverson was finally allowed to proceed, laying out the bill spectacularly. He articulated his points perfectly, backing them up with medical research and science. He referenced the high suicide rate among transitioners, underscoring why the bill was important for their protection.

Then came the amendments. Oh, the amendments! The Democrats attempted to amend the bill nineteen times. Each proposed amendment would lead to what seemed like hours of endless debate. Their arguments were ridiculous! It reminded me of the night I testified on the READER Act and Rep. Talarico tried to argue what sexually explicit meant. Their arguments contained no substance.

I did not attend the proceedings in person on May 12th, but watched the live video feed at home. I was provoked in my spirit when the Democrats tried to amend the bill the fourth or fifth time. I knew this was simply the enemy trying to hold up our bill. God had declared on April 25th that the bill would pass, and the enemy needed to get out of our way!

This is when I engaged the ekklesia via our Signal chat. Several apostles had attended the night of prayer and worship on April 25th and stayed involved with SB 14 in the following weeks. I had added these apostles to the Signal chat with our convoy members, so I was able to engage them for legislative prayer quickly.

As amendments six through ten came up, I instructed the apostles to issue their apostolic decrees in Signal as the other convoy members seated in the House gallery came into agreement. One of the apostles, Kyle Byrd, who was in attendance, held up his phone and walked around the House gallery playing our decrees out loud as they came across in the form of voice memos.

148

As each member of the House rose to speak in favor of an amendment, we would bind their words to the roof of their mouths, and we would reverse their words with our decrees. This went on for over an hour.

When we finally got to the tenth amendment, we declared confusion over the enemy and decreed that none of their amendments would receive any further support. As amendments ten through seventeen rolled out, we noticed that each one garnered less and less support. When we reached the eighteenth and nineteenth amendments, we noticed that the opposition's voice had lowered to a whimper. They knew they had been defeated.

The protestors left the gallery. They knew they had lost, too. No more amendments were offered, the vote was taken, and the bill passed! God won the day just like He said He would! What amazed me the most was the temperament of Dr. Oliverson. He stood there for hours, taking on amendment after amendment, never showing any signs of wavering or weakness — not one single time. I thought, *God, you raised up this man for this hour. Here is an example of a modern-day Daniel, full of the wisdom of God in a Babylonian system.*

After our win on SB 14, the other bills in the Millstone Package fell in line. We saw the passage of six more bills that protected Texas kids. HB 900 passed, getting the dirty books out of public schools.

SB 15 passed, banning biological men from competing in women's collegiate sports. SB 12 passed, banning drag queen shows in front of children. HB 4520 passed, increasing consequences for educators who sexually harm children. HB 1181 passed, restricting access to sexual websites for minors. And SB 1527 passed, providing a criminal penalty for sexually grooming children. We also saw ten other pro-conservative bills pass that increased border security, defended gun rights, brought medical freedom, and addressed election integrity.

For conservatives, the 88th Legislative Session was one of the biggest successes we have ever had. In a House full of RINOs and Democrats, God sovereignly moved and performed His wonders. Surprisingly, several Democrats came over to our side and voted in favor of SB 14, risking retribution from their own party. Houston Representative Shawn Thierry was one of the Democrats who made headlines for voting in favor of SB 14 and influencing her colleagues to do the same.[3]

The 88th Legislature was a massive win for North Texas Conservatives and all conservatives in our state. We took fourteen busloads to the Capitol on twelve separate missions. We raised $22,625 in bus sponsorships. We put a total of 600 boots on the ground. We performed over 800 office visits. We made thousands of phone calls and emails and lobbied over 84,000 hours during the session. This resulted in seventeen conservative bills passing into law. After the cancel culture attack of 2021, the arduous two-year journey of rebuilding our PAC resulted in a glorious testimony of God's redeeming grace and overcoming love.

The Bible is so true when it says, "With man this is impossible, but with God all things are possible" (Matthew 19:26). We witnessed this firsthand in the 88th Texas Legislature. I choose to give God all the glory because I know we didn't accomplish this through our hand but through God's power. He was the one who gave us the Big, Hairy, Audacious Goal (BHAG®), and He was the one who downloaded the strategy for achieving it. To God be all the glory; great things He has done.

Chapter 10

The Python Around Texas

Our final trip to the Capitol took place on May 16th. I honestly wasn't sure I felt like returning to the Capitol after the transurrection. However, God needed me there.

My friend, Audrey Werner, reached out to me and asked if I could participate in a Reverse the Kinsey Decision Day at the Capitol on May 16th. I met Audrey for the first time on our April 25th bus trip to the Capitol, and I was impressed with her presentation at the "Stop Sexualizing Texas Kids" forum that day. Audrey is the author of the book *10 Tips on How Not to Talk to Your Kids About Sex* and is the founder and president of *The Matthew XVIII Group*.

Her ministry uses the Matthew 18:15-17 process to approach Christian leaders who are using Dr. Alfred Kinsey's fraudulent and criminal science on sex education. Her hope is that once his junk research is exposed, Kinsey's works can be purged from Christian resources.

Audrey had to educate me on who Alfred Kinsey was. Dr. Kinsey was a sexual revolutionary in the 40s and 50s who tried to rewrite the definition of marriage (and succeeded, I might add). He was the advisor to the creation of the Model Penal Code, which eliminated and weakened fifty-two laws that once protected marriage, women, and children.

Kinsey's junk research on "normal" human sexual behavior became the model for sex education in American public schools starting in the 60s. Most of his findings were based on 18,000 interviews he conducted with sexual perverts. 5,300 of his subjects were white males, of which 2,446 were convicts, 1,003 were homosexuals, 50 were transvestites, 117 were mentally ill, 342 were other, and 650 were sexually abused boys. His other primary source for his study was Von Balluseck, a Nazi pedophile who practiced sexual acts on Polish children in German concentration camps.

After a decade of research, Kinsey claimed that his findings reflected "normal sexuality" in the American male population. Kinsey's research was widely accepted because Indiana University sponsored him. Kinsey's research ignited the Sexual Revolution of the 1960s through his publication of *Sexual Behavior in the Human Male* in 1948 and *Sexual Behavior in the Human Female* in 1953.[1]

154

In addition to re-writing the definition of marriage, Kinsey also re-wrote our nation's penal code. In 1997, biographer James Jones revealed that Kinsey's mission was to end the sexual repression of the English-American common law traditions. Virtually every page of Kinsey's research touched on some section of the legal code.

The Model Penal Code was drafted in 1955 based on Kinsey's findings. Sodomy and related offenses, including pedophilia with children as young as ten, were lowered from a felony to a misdemeanor. States soon adopted Kinsey's research into their penal codes, and within a matter of decades, all fifty states changed from common law to the Model Penal Code.

This change had a profound effect on American morality. Men who raped and preyed on children were no longer deemed "criminals," but simply "actors" performing their normal sexual desires. The definition of "adult" now included children for purposes of sex. Abused and violated women and children were no longer "victims," but simply "complainants" seeking an audience. Justice was no longer meted out by a jury of one's peers, but by social science "experts." Predators no longer received penalties for their actions, but legal protection.

The creation of multiple degrees for sex crimes negated the felony penalty. And, sex education in public schools, based on Kinsey's research, was recommended as the primary crime prevention measure.[2]

Texas followed suit in adopting the Model Penal Code in 1973. This decision took place on May 16, 1973, when the Criminal Jurisprudence Committee met in the Old Supreme Court Room at the State Capitol.[3] When Audrey learned that the 50th anniversary of this decision was coming up on May 16th, she felt prompted by the Holy Spirit to hold a *Reverse the Kinsey Decision Day* at the Capitol. She asked me to speak at the event along with Christian activist Jaco Booyens, who had just produced the movie *Sex Nation*. I prayed and asked the Lord about it. Sensing His strong leading, I told Audrey I would speak at the event.

I brought a team of intercessors with me that day because I knew prayer was the key to overturning Kinsey's demonic doctrine. Our team arrived before the event began, and we prayed over the room. We anointed the furnishings, including a bookcase containing bound copies of the 1973 Kinsey decision. We also anointed the Supreme Court bench, which displayed the inscription "SICUT PATRIBUS SIT DEUS NOBIS," which means "God be with us as He was with our fathers" and is found in 1 Kings 8:57.

The program began at 2 p.m. and Audrey was first up. She spoke on the history of the Kinsey doctrine and how his immorality had shifted America away from God. She also addressed the Model Penal Code and how Texas adopted it into our law system in 1973.

Next up was Jaco Booyens. He spoke about the attack on traditional marriage and took us back to the foundation of God's original design for men. He said that a man of God is a force to be reckoned with. He reminded us that marriage was one of the only things to make it out of the Garden of Eden and that we needed to protect it.

Finally, it was my turn to speak. I spoke straight from my heart as I talked about how the enemy had targeted my generation, Gen X, from birth. I got very emotional when I realized I was standing in the same room where Rep. Sarah Weddington served on the Criminal Jurisprudence Committee in 1973.

For those unfamiliar with Sarah Weddington, she was the attorney who represented Jane Roe in the case that became known as *Roe vs. Wade*. The case passed the U.S. Supreme Court in January 1973 by a 7-2 majority, overturning Texas' abortion law and legalizing abortion throughout the United States.[4] Sarah was elected to the 63rd Texas Legislature before *Roe vs. Wade* was decided and served on the Criminal Jurisprudence Committee on May 16th, the day the Kinsey doctrine was adopted into Texas' penal code.

Tears began to roll down my face as I realized that what happened in this room fifty years ago was meant to stop my generation from fulfilling their purpose in God. I have always been passionate about

Generation X. After I was born again at age twelve, and filled with the Holy Spirit at thirteen, the Lord laid a deep burden on my heart to reach my generation. I had always felt that my generation was lost. I believed they only gave us the label "X" because they didn't know what to do with us.

We were the analog to the digital generation. We were the first generation to use computers. We were also the latchkey generation. Ours was the generation that witnessed the divorce rate skyrocket. This caused us to be a disillusioned generation and a lost generation. Ours was the generation to experience fatherlessness on an unprecedented scale.

My heart has always felt broken for my generation, and I have always wanted to reach them with the love and compassion of Christ. My life turned around radically when I met the Lord as a teenager. He placed a fire within me that burned deep in my soul, and I have longed to reach my generation with that fire ever since.

As I spoke about Generation X in the old Supreme Court room that day, the passion of the Lord stirred within my heart. SB 14 had just passed four days earlier, and the fire from that victory was fresh in my soul. As I concluded my remarks, I told the audience that we would enter a time of prayer to reverse the Kinsey decision over our state.

As we moved into corporate worship, someone blew the shofar, and I felt the presence of God. After worshipping with a song or two, I prayed over the Kinsey decision, leading the audience in several prayer decrees. I then handed the prayer meeting over to other intercessors on my team. As they prayed, Apostle Kyle sensed we should go behind the Supreme Court bench and stand behind the chairs. I didn't sense otherwise, so I agreed, and we walked behind the bench.

Apostle Kyle, my father, and I stood behind the three chairs lined up on the bench, and we continued to pray. I then sensed that I was supposed to sit in the middle chair as a prophetic act, declaring that Jesus was taking his rightful seat as King of Kings and Lord of Lords over Texas.

If you are unfamiliar with prophetic acts, they are acts done in the natural realm under the inspiration of the Holy Spirit that support God's workings in the spiritual realm. These acts open up great power, presence, and victory in the natural realm and change outcomes.

Examples of this can be found in scripture, such as when Ezekiel had to lie on his left side for 390 days and his right side for forty days to bear the punishment of Israel and Judah in Ezekiel 4. Also, when Agabus bound Paul's hands symbolizing his capture if he went to Rome in Acts 21:11.

As I sat down in the middle chair, I immediately saw in the spirit realm tons of snakes slithering under my feet beneath the bench. I could sense that the deep darkness and deception that had influenced the 1973 Kinsey decision was still in the room.

I then heard Apostle Kyle decree that the darkness was leaving and the light was returning to our state. As he spoke these words, a *ruach* wind blew into the room and knocked me out of my chair. *Ruach* is the Hebrew word for spirit, breath, or wind.[5] The term refers to God as a breath, wind, or life force that sustains all living things. When the *ruach* blows into a room, it is usually because God is breathing life into something. At least, this has been my experience.

The *ruach* blew into the room as we prayed because God was reversing the spirit of death released there in 1973.

As I lay on the floor under the power of God, I felt a python spirit coil itself around my body and start to squeeze. If you are unfamiliar with a python spirit, it is a demon in Satan's army intent on snatching the *ruach* from God's people. Translated as "spirit of divination" in Acts 16:16, the python was a mythical serpent said to have guarded the oracle of Delphi and was slain by Apollo.[6] The oracle of Delphi, considered by some as the most famous ancient oracle, was believed to deliver prophecies from the Greek god Apollo. These prophecies were given in his temple at Delphi, located on the slopes of Mt. Parnassus above the Corinthian Gulf.[7]

Paul encountered this spirit in Philippi on his way to prayer one day when he was met by a slave girl who brought her masters much profit by fortune-telling. The Bible says that she followed Paul, saying, "These men are the servants of the Most High God, who proclaim to us the way of salvation." She did this for many days.

Finally, Paul, greatly annoyed, turned and said to the spirit, "I command you in the name of Jesus Christ to come out of her. And he came out that very hour" (Acts 16:16-18).

The python spirit I was now encountering began to squeeze tightly around my body. I could barely breathe. The team continued to pray as I wrestled with this spirit. Then, in the spirit realm, the Holy Spirit showed me an outline of the state of Texas. Wrapped around our state, I saw this python spirit. It was huge, and it was squeezing the life out of God's people. I could sense that this demonic spirit was preventing the move of the Holy Spirit in the Church and the government. The Lord then took a sword and began to cut the python spirit off me and the state of Texas. I then came out of the encounter.

It wasn't until a month later that the Lord revealed to me what this python spirit was in my state. I was shocked to find out that it had been set in place during the founding of Texas, and that God was about to deal with it!

We had completed our divinely appointed task for the 88th Legislative session, but now God was about to call us, His ekklesia, to another assignment. It was time to "command the foreword" over Texas.

To Be Continued . . .

Conclusion

I hope you enjoyed reading my book. This is the first in a series of books designed to express what God is doing through His Daniels in this hour. In my next book, I will be sharing about the Daniel calling on this generation. I will include my story about God's call on my life at an early age and draw a parallel between my pursuit of God and this generation's pursuit of God.

We live in historic times where we will see a Daniel generation arise and defeat evil in a single lifetime. Don't be surprised when a generation that has been greatly confused and underestimated rises up and becomes God's chosen army in the earth.

We are about to witness the greatest influx of kingdom warriors the church has ever seen. Are you ready to spiritually father and mother them? Are you ready to run with them? I hope so because what God is about to do is unstoppable, and we need to steward their giftings and callings. Get ready! God is about to rock our world.

Connect With Us!

Your input matters greatly to us! At Daniel Nation, our mission is to empower individuals with a deep understanding of their First Amendment rights and guide them in applying these rights in their lives.

Our approach involves comprehensive training in grassroots activism, advocating for positions, crafting legislative policies, interfacing with lawmakers, pursuing political office, fostering alliances, establishing organizations, and a myriad of other impactful avenues!

To arrange a training session with Brandon, kindly reach out to him via email at brandon@danielnation.com, or give him a call at (214) 649-0623. We eagerly await your connection!

Please check out our resources on our website at **www.danielnation.com.**

Please follow us on social media at:

Facebook: facebook.com/DanielNationPBC

Twitter/X: x.com/DanielNationPBC

Instagram: instagram.com/DanielNationPBC

Gab: gab.com/DanielNationPBC

YouTube: youtube.com/@DanielNationPBC

Please help us spread the word about *Daniel Nation* by leaving a 5-star review on Amazon.com. Click this QR code to leave a 5-star review on Amazon.com or visit my page at: www.amazon.com/author/brandonlburden/.

The more 5-star reviews we get, the better our book will rank. And, please tell a friend to purchase our book!

Biography

Brandon Burden wears many hats — a Christian leader, pastor, businessman, and conservative activist. He also holds a real estate broker's license in Texas and leads Daniel Nation, a public benefit corporation. His engagement with the community spans years, dating back to his 2017 involvement in Frisco's city council elections, where his campaign initiated vital discussions on reining in soaring property taxes. His efforts culminated in the passage of the Texas Property Tax Reform & Transparency Act of 2019, impacting the entire state.

As a founding member of Frisco Conservatives PAC and later serving as Chairman until 2023, Brandon steered the group to remarkable success. Under his leadership, the PAC empowered 49 conservative candidates in the 2020 election and raised substantial funds supporting President Donald J. Trump's Texas re-election campaign. The PAC's platform attracted influential speakers like Congresswoman Marjorie Taylor Greene, Lt. Col. Allen West, Dinesh D'Souza, David J. Harris, Jr., and other prominent figures, fostering dialogue and political engagement.

Transitioning to North Texas Conservatives in 2022, the organization pivoted its mission towards proactive advocacy. They orchestrated a significant movement, escorting 600 activists to the State Capitol, resulting in the passage of 17 pro-conservative bills during the 88th Texas Legislative session.

Brandon's fervor lies in empowering individuals to embody Christ's voice in society, reclaiming cultural ground relinquished by the church. He champions the synergy between apostolic and prophetic ministries joining hands with dedicated grassroots patriots as instrumental in reshaping America's future. He envisions a collaborative approach between faith and activism — a formula, he believes, capable of toppling oppressive forces and reclaiming America for God.

Beyond his impactful pursuits, Brandon shares a fulfilling life with his wife, Willy, since 2004, and their four cherished children. In his leisure, he indulges in real estate ventures and cherishes family travels to exquisite destinations. Brandon eagerly anticipates the unfolding of God's plans for the future, believing in the transformative power of united faith and grassroots activism.

NOTES

CHAPTER 2

[1] "2015 Comprehensive Plan." Frisco Texas. August 4, 2015 https://www.friscotexas.gov/1064/2015-Comprehensive-Plan

CHAPTER 3

[1] Price, Dr. Paula. 2006. *The Prophet's Dictionary: The Ultimate Guide to Supernatural Wisdom*. Whitaker House.

[2] Ibid.

[3] Cunningham, Loren, and Janice Rogers. 1989. *Making Jesus Lord: The Dynamic Power of Laying Down Your Rights*. YWAM Publishing.

[4] Wallnau, Lance, and Bill Johnson. 2013. *Invading Babylon: The 7 Mountain Mandate*. Destiny Image Publishers.

[5] "Radah." Bible Hub. Accessed August 23, 2023. https://biblehub.com/hebrew/7287.htm.

CHAPTER 5

[1] "Ronald Reagan." AZ Quotes. Accessed September 14, 2023. https://www.azquotes.com/quote/519272.

CHAPTER 6

[1] "Kim Clement Trump Prophecies in 2007 | Prophetic Rewind | House of Destiny Network." Kim Clement. November 13, 2022. Video, https://youtu.be/k5XEQ-RhRqY?si=oLOPNmCWt10UcGB8.

[2] Ibid.

[3] Addison, Brandi. "Frisco Pastor Urges Followers to Keep Guns Loaded, Stock up on Food and Water before Biden Inauguration." *The Dallas Morning News* (Dallas), January 13, 2021. https://www.dallasnews.com/news/politics/2021/01/14/frisco-pastor-urges-followers-to-help-trump-stay-in-office-and-keep-guns-loaded-before-biden-inauguration/.

[4] Addison, Brandi. "Frisco Pastor's 'Dangerous' Words, Far-right Views Don't Reflect Their City, Conservative Leaders Say." *The Dallas Morning News* (Dallas), January 20, 2021. https://www.dallasnews.com/news/politics/2021/01/21/frisco-pastors-dangerous-words-far-right-views-at-kingdomlife-dont-reflect-their-city-conservative-leaders-say/.

[5] Addison, Brandi. "Frisco Pastor Temporarily Out as Chairman of Conservative PAC after His Comments on Trump, Guns." The Dallas Morning News (Dallas), January 29, 2021. https://www.dallasnews.com/news/politics/2021/01/29/frisco-pastors-conservative-pac-loses-board-members-in-the-fallout-from-his-comments-about-trump-guns/.

6 "Public Statement from Pastor Brandon Burden of KingdomLife Church Regarding Media Controversy." Kingdom Life Design. January 25, 2021. Video, https://youtu.be/zb-3KjEf8fg.

7 Addison, Brandi. "Frisco Pastor Promotes False Claims of Stolen Election with Event at His Church This Week." *The Dallas Morning News* (Dallas), February 23, 2021. https://www.dallasnews.com/news/politics/2021/02/23/frisco-pastor-promotes-false-claims-of-stolen-election-with-event-at-his-church-this-week/.

8 Closson, David. "Christian Nationalism? The Left's Latest Attempt to Silence Believers." Family Research Council. July 31, 2019. https://www.frc.org/get.cfm?i=WA19G54.

9 Addison, Brandi. "Marjorie Taylor Greene? No Thanks, Says Billboard Funded by Frisco Residents." *The Dallas Morning News* (Dallas), November 19, 2021. https://www.dallasnews.com/news/politics/2021/11/19/marjorie-taylor-greene-no-thanks-says-billboard-funded-by-frisco-residents/.

CHAPTER 7

1 Pollock, Cassandra. "Speaker Dade Phelan Shakes up Texas House Leadership with New Chairs on Key Committees." The Texas Tribune. February 4, 2021. https://www.texastribune.org/2021/02/04/texas-house-dade-phelan-committee-chairs/.

2 "2023-2024 Legislative Priorities." Republican Party of Texas. Accessed August 16, 2023. https://texasgop.org/priorities/.

3 Nash, Clay. "Declaration of Dependence by Patriotic Citizens of the United States of America as Ekklesia E Pluribus Unum." July 4, 2022. https://www.claynash.org/uploads/1/3/0/7/130727 692/declaration_of_dependence_rev_9.3.pdf.

4 Patterson, Jared. "HB 900." Texas Legislature Online. Accessed September 27, 2023. https://capitol.texas.gov/BillLookup/History.aspx?L egSess=88R&Bill=HB900

CHAPTER 8

1 Campbell, Donna. "SB 14." Texas Legislature Online. Accessed October 2, 2023. https://capitol.texas.gov/BillLookup/History.aspx?L egSess=88R&Bill=SB14.

2 Leiman, Sid Z. "Jewish Religious Year." Britannica. October 15, 2023. https://www.britannica.com/topic/Jewish-religious-year.

3 "Waldseemüller, Martin." Encyclopedia.Com. May 29, 2018. https://www.encyclopedia.com/people/science-and-technology/geography-biographies/martin-waldseemuller.

4 "Ekklesia." Bible Study Tools. Accessed August 23, 2023. https://www.biblestudytools.com/lexicons/greek/kj v/ekklesia.html

CHAPTER 9

1 Nguyen, Alex, and Sneha Dey. "Protesters Evicted from Texas Capitol as Clash between LGBTQ Residents and GOP Leaders Escalates." The Texas Tribune (Austin), May 2, 2023. https://www.texastribune.org/2023/05/02/texas-trans-kids-health-care-ban/.

2 Burden, Larry. 2012. *The Orphan Heart: Restoring True Sonship.* Insight International, Inc.

3 "Rep. Shawn Thierry SB 14 Vote Brings Praise, Blowback." Defender Network. May 24, 2023. https://defendernetwork.com/news/local-state/rep-shawn-thierry-sb-14-vote-brings-praise-blowback/.

CHAPTER 10

1 Jeffrey, Dr. Linda. "Restoring Legal Protections for Women And Children: A Historical Analysis of The States Criminal Codes." *American Legislative Exchange Council: The State Factor* (Washington, D.C.), April 2, 2004.

2 Ibid.

3 "Reforming the Penal Law; Enacting a New Penal Code Setting Out General Principles, Defining Offenses, and Affixing Punishments, Making Necessary Conforming Amendments to outside Law; Repealing Replaced Law." Legislative Reference Library of Texas. May 16, 1973. https://lrl.texas.gov/legis/billsearch/BillDetails.cfm?legSession=63-

0&billtypeDetail=SB&billNumberDetail=34&billSuffix Detail=.

4 Wikipedia. 2023. "Sarah Weddington." Wikimedia Foundation. Last modified September 27, 2023. https://en.wikipedia.org/wiki/Sarah_Weddington.

5 "Ruach." Bible Hub. Accessed September 2, 2023. https://biblehub.com/hebrew/7308.htm.

6 Wikipedia. 2023. "Python (Mythology)." Wikimedia Foundation. Last modified October 7, 2023. https://en.wikipedia.org/wiki/Python_(mythology).

7 Wikipedia. 2023. "Pythia." Wikimedia Foundation. Last modified October 4, 2023. https://en.wikipedia.org/wiki/Pythia.

Made in the USA
Columbia, SC
06 December 2024

48596529R00096